LEVEL 1

Jacob's Ladder

READING COMPREHENSION PROGRAM

Grades 2–3

LEVEL 1

Jacob's Ladder
READING COMPREHENSION PROGRAM
Grades 2–3

(Second Edition)

EDITED BY:
JOYCE VANTASSEL-BASKA
TAMRA STAMBAUGH

Center for Gifted Education,
The College of William and Mary

Contributing Authors
(in alphabetical order):
Heather French
Paula Ginsburgh
Tamra Stambaugh
Joyce VanTassel-Baska

Special Acknowledgements:
Kathryn Holt

Funded by the United States Department of
Education, Javits Program

PRUFROCK PRESS INC.
WACO, TEXAS

Edited by Lacy Compton
Production Design by Marjorie Parker

ISBN-13: 978-1-59363-350-9
ISBN-10: 1-59363-350-5

Prufrock Press Inc.
P.O. Box 8813
Waco, TX 76714-8813
Phone: (800) 998-2208
Fax: (800) 240-0333
http://www.prufrock.com

Contents

Part I:
Teachers' Guide to Jacob's Ladder Reading Comprehension Program

Introduction to *Jacob's Ladder, Level 1*

Jacob's Ladder, Level 1 is a supplemental reading program that implements targeted readings from short stories, poetry, and nonfiction sources. With this program, students engage in an inquiry process that moves from lower order to higher order thinking skills. Starting with basic literary understanding, students learn to critically analyze texts by determining implications and consequences, generalizations, main ideas, and/or creative synthesis. Suggested for students in third grade to enhance reading comprehension and critical thinking, *Jacob's Ladder, Level 1* tasks are organized into four skill ladders: A–D. Each ladder focuses on a different skill. Students "climb" each ladder by answering lower level questions before moving to higher level questions or rungs at the top of each ladder. Each ladder stands alone and focuses on a separate critical thinking component in reading.

Ladder A focuses on implications and consequences. By leading students through sequencing and cause and effect activities, students learn to draw implications and consequences from readings. Ladder B focuses on making generalizations. Students first learn to provide details and examples, then move to classifying and organizing those details in order to make generalizations. Ladder C focuses on themes. Students begin by identifying setting and characters and then make inferences about the literary situation. Ladder D focuses on creative synthesis by leading students through paraphrasing and summarizing activities. Table 1 provides a visual representation of the four ladders and corresponding objectives for each ladder and rung.

TABLE 1
Goals and Objectives of *Jacob's Ladder* by Ladder and Rung

A3: Consequences and Implications	B3: Generalizations	C3: Theme/Concept	D3: Creative Synthesis
Students will be able to predict character actions, story outcomes, and make real-world forecasts.	Students will be able to make general statements about a reading and/or an idea within the reading, using data to support their statements.	Students will be able to identify a major idea or theme common throughout the text.	Students will create something new using what they have learned from the reading and their synopses.
A2: Cause and Effect	**B2: Classifications**	**C2: Inference**	**D2: Summarizing**
Students will be able to identify and predict relationships between character behavior and story events, and their effects upon other characters or events.	Students will be able to categorize different aspects of the text or identify and sort categories from a list of topics or details.	Students will be able to use textual clues to read between the lines and make judgments about specific textual events, ideas, or character analysis.	Students will be able to provide a synopsis of text sections.
A1: Sequencing	**B1: Details**	**C1: Literary Elements**	**D1: Paraphrasing**
Students will be able to list, in order of importance or occurrence in the text, specific events or plot summaries.	Students will be able to list specific details or recall facts related to the text or generate a list of ideas about a specific topic or character.	Students will be able to identify and explain specific story elements such as character, setting, or poetic device.	Students will be able to restate lines read using their own words.
Ladder A	Ladder B	Ladder C	Ladder D

The *Jacob's Ladder* series consists of three levels: 1, 2 and 3. All three levels contain 10 short stories, 10 poems, 6 nonfiction selections, and 2 commensurate ladders for each selection, with the exception of Level 1 in which some reading selections have one ladder. *Jacob's Ladder 1* is recommended for students in grade 3, *Jacob's Ladder 2* is recommended for students in grade 4, and *Jacob's Ladder 3* is recommended for students in grade 5. However, teachers may find that they want to vary usage beyond the recommended levels, depending on student abilities. For example, Level 1 can be used with students in grades 2 and 3, Level 2 can be used with grades 4 and 5, and Level 3 can be used with middle school students. Anecdotal evidence suggests that the curriculum has been successfully implemented with precocious primary students, as well as less experienced middle school students.

Ladder A:
Focus on Implications and Consequences

The goal of Ladder A is to develop prediction and forecasting skills by encouraging students to make connections among the information provided. Starting with sequencing, students learn to recognize basic types of change that occur within a text. Through identifying cause and effect relationships, students then can judge the impact of certain events. Finally, through recognizing consequences and implications, students predict future events as logical and identify both short- and long-term consequences by judging probable outcomes based on data provided. The rungs are as follows:

- **Ladder A, Rung 1, Sequencing**: The lowest rung on the ladder, sequencing, requires students to organize a set of information in order, based on their reading (e.g., List the steps of a recipe in order).

- **Ladder A, Rung 2, Cause and Effect**: The middle rung, cause and effect, requires students to think about relationships and identify what causes certain effects and/or what effects were brought about because of certain causes (e.g., What causes a cake to rise in the oven? What effect does the addition of egg yolks have on a batter?).

- **Ladder A, Rung 3, Consequences and Implications**: The highest rung on Ladder A requires students to think about both short-term and long-term events that may happen as a result of an effect they have identified (e.g., What are the short-term and long-term consequences of baking at home?). Students learn to draw consequences and implications from text for application in the real world.

Ladder B: Focus on Generalizations

The goal of Ladder B is to help students develop deductive reasoning skills, moving from the concrete elements in a story to abstract ideas.

Students begin by learning the importance of concrete details and how they can be organized. By the top rung, students are able to make general statements spanning a topic or concept. The rungs are as follows:

- **Ladder B, Rung 1, Details**: The lowest rung on Ladder B, details/examples, requires students to list examples or details from what they have read and/or to list examples they know from the real world or have read about (e.g., Make a list of examples of transportation. Write as many as you can think of in 2 minutes).

- **Ladder B, Rung 2, Classifications**: The middle rung of Ladder B focuses on students' ability to categorize examples and details based on characteristics (e.g., How might we categorize the modes of transportation you identified?). This activity builds students' skills in categorization and classification.

- **Ladder B, Rung 3, Generalizations**: The highest rung on Ladder B, generalization, requires students to use the list and categories generated at Rungs 1 and 2 to develop 2–3 general statements that apply to *all* of their examples (e.g., Write three statements about transportation).

Ladder C: Focus on Themes

The goal of Ladder C is to develop literary analysis skills based on an understanding of literary elements. After completing Ladder C, students state main themes and ideas of text after identifying setting, characters, and the context of the piece. The rungs are as follows:

- **Ladder C, Rung 1, Literary Elements**: While working on Rung 1, students identify and/or describe the setting or situation in which the reading occurs. This rung also requires students to develop an understanding of given characters by identifying qualities he or she possesses and comparing these qualities to other characters they have encountered in their reading (e.g., In *Goldilocks and the Three Bears*, what is the situation in which Goldilocks finds herself? What qualities do you admire in Goldilocks? What qualities do you find problematic? How is she similar or different from other fairy tale characters you have encountered?).

- **Ladder C, Rung 2, Inference**: Inference serves as the middle rung of this ladder and requires students to think through a situation in the text and come to a conclusion based on the information and clues provided (e.g., What evidence exists that Goldilocks ate the porridge? What inferences can you make about the bear's subsequent action?).

- **Ladder C, Rung 3, Theme/Concept**: As the highest rung of Ladder C, this step requires students to state the central idea or theme for a reading. This exercise asks students to explain an idea from the reading that best states what the text means (e.g., How would you rename the fairy tale? Why? What is the overall theme of *Goldilocks and the Three Bears*? Which of the following morals apply to the fairy tale? Why or why not?).

Ladder D: Focus on Creative Synthesis

The goal of Ladder D is to help students develop skills in creative synthesis in order to foster students' creation of new material based on information from the reading. It moves from the level of restating ideas to creating new ideas about a topic or concept. The rungs are as follows:

- **Ladder D, Rung 1, Paraphrasing**: The lowest rung on Ladder D is paraphrasing. This rung requires students to restate a short passage using their own words (e.g., Rewrite the following quotation in your own words: "But as soon as [the slave] came near to Androcles, he recognized his friend, and fawned upon him, and licked his hands like a friendly dog. The emperor, surprised at this, summoned Androcles to him, who told the whole story. Whereupon the slave was pardoned and freed, and the Lion let loose to his native forest.").

- **Ladder D, Rung 2, Summarizing**: Summarizing, the middle rung, requires students to summarize larger sections of text by selecting the most important key points within a passage (e.g., Choose one section of the story and summarize it in five sentences).

- **Ladder D, Rung 3, Creative Synthesis**: The highest rung on Ladder D requires students to create something new using what they have learned from the reading and their synopses of it (e.g., Write another fable about the main idea you identified for this fable, using characters, setting, and a plot of your choice).

Process Skills

Along with the four goals addressed by the ladders, a fifth goal, process skills, is incorporated in the *Jacob's Ladder* curriculum. The aim of this goal is to promote learning through interaction and discussion of reading material in the classroom. After completing the ladders and following guidelines for discussion and teacher feedback, students will be able to:

- articulate their understanding of a reading passage using textual support,

- engage in proper dialogue about the meaning of a selection, and

- discuss varied ideas about intention of a passage both orally and in writing.

Reading Genres and Selections

The reading selections include three major genres: short stories (fables, myths, short stories, and essays), poetry, and nonfiction. In Level 1, each reading within a genre has been carefully selected or tailored for third-grade reading accessibility and interest. The stories and poems for the *Jacob's Ladder* curriculum at each grade level were chosen with three basic criteria in mind: (1) concrete to abstract development, (2) level of vocabulary, and (3) age-appropriate themes. The readings and exercises are designed to move students forward in their abstract thinking processes by promoting critical and creative thinking. The vocabulary in each reading is grade-level appropriate, however when new or unfamiliar words are encountered, they should be covered in class before readings and ladder questions are assigned. Themes also are appropriate to the students' ages at each grade level and were chosen to complement themes typically seen in texts for each particular level. The short stories, poetry, and nonfiction readings with corresponding ladder sets are delineated in Part II. Table 2 outlines all Level 1 readings by genre.

Rationale

Constructing meaning of the written word is one of the earliest tasks required of students in schools. This skill occupies the central place in the curriculum at the elementary level. Yet, approaches to teaching reading comprehension often are "skill and drill," using worksheets on low-level reading material. As a result, students frequently are unable to transfer these skills from exercise pages and apply them to new higher level reading material.

The time expended to ensure that students become autonomous and advanced readers would suggest the need for a methodology that deliberately moves students from simple to complex reading skills with grade-

TABLE 2
Reading Selections by Genre

Fables and Myths	Poetry	Nonfiction
The Ant and the Dove	Artist	Ancient Rome
The Crow and the Pitcher	City	The Circle of Life
Daedalus and Icarus	Delilah	Geometry All Around Us
The Dog and His Reflection	Fog	The Industrial Revolution
The Fisherman and His Wife	Imagination	What's the Chance?
The Judge	Remembering	A World of Resources
The Lion and the Gnat	A Rose	
The Mice in Council	Under My Bed	
The North Wind and the Sun	Windy Nights	
The Tap Dancer	Winter Horses	

appropriate texts. Such a learning approach to reading skill development ensures that students can traverse easily from basic comprehension skills to higher level critical reading skills, while using the same reading stimulus to navigate this transition. Reading comprehension is enhanced by instructional scaffolding, moving students from lower order to higher order thinking, using strategies and processes to help students analyze passages (Fielding & Pearson, 1994; Villaume & Brabham, 2002). In addition, teachers who emphasize higher order thinking through questions and tasks such as those at the higher rungs of each ladder promote greater reading growth (Knapp et al., 1995; Taylor, Pearson, Peterson, & Rodriguez, 2003).

Jacob's Ladder was written in response to teacher findings that students needed additional scaffolding to consistently work at higher levels of thinking in reading. In addition, an analysis of reading reform curriculum by the American Federation of Teachers (AFT, 1998) shows that only two of the recommended curricula posit a research base and a focus on critical thinking skills in reading. Similarly, Tivnan and Hemphill (2005) studied reading reform curricula in Title I schools and found that none of the reading programs studied emphasized skills beyond basic phonemic awareness, fluency, or limited comprehension. Therefore, supplementary curriculum that focuses on higher level thinking skills is needed.

The *Jacob's Ladder* program is a compilation of the instructional scaffolding and reading exercises necessary to aid students in their journey toward becoming critical readers. Students learn concept development skills through learning to generalize, predicting and forecasting skills through delineating implications of events, and literary analysis skills through discerning textual meaning. The questions and tasks for each reading are open-ended, as this type of approach to responding to literature improves performance on comprehension tests (Guthrie, Schafer, & Huang, 2001). Progressing through the hierarchy of skills also requires students to re-read the text, thereby improving metacomprehension accuracy (Rawson, Dunlosky, & Thiede, 2000).

Research Base

A quasi-experimental study was conducted using *Jacob's Ladder* as a supplementary program for students in Title I schools, grades 3–5. After professional development occurred, experimental teachers were instructed to implement the *Jacob's Ladder* curriculum in addition to their basal reading series and guided reading groups. Teachers in the control group taught their district-adopted textbook reading series as the main curriculum.

Findings from this study (N = 495) suggest that when compared to students who used the basal reader only, those students who were exposed to the *Jacob's Ladder* curriculum showed significant gains in reading comprehension and critical thinking. Likewise, students who used the curriculum showed significant and important growth on curriculum-based assessments that included determining implications/consequences, making inferences, outlining themes and generalizations, and applying creative synthesis. Students reported greater interest in reading and eluded that the curriculum made them "think harder." Teachers reported more in-depth student discussion and personal growth in the ability to ask open-ended questions when reading (Stambaugh, 2008).

Implementation Considerations

Teachers need to consider certain issues when implementing the *Jacob's Ladder* curriculum. Although the program is targeted for promising students who need more exposure to higher level thinking skills in reading, the program may be suitable for learners who are functioning above or below grade level.

As modeling, coaching, and feedback appear to enhance student growth in reading and writing (Pressley et al., 2001; Taylor, Peterson, Pearson, & Rodriguez, 2002), it is recommended that teachers review how to complete the task ladders with the entire class at least once, outlining expectations and record-keeping tasks, as well as modeling the process prior to assigning small-group or independent work. Students should complete the ladder tasks on their own paper or on the template provided in Appendix B. As students gain more confidence in the curriculum, the teacher should allow more independent work coupled with small group or paired discussion, and then whole-group sharing with teacher feedback.

Completing these activities in dyads or small groups will facilitate discussions that stress collaborative reasoning, thereby fostering greater engagement and higher level thinking (Chin, Anderson, & Waggoner, 2001; Pressley et al., 2001; Taylor et al., 2002). The stories and accompanying ladder questions and activities also may be organized into a reading center in the classroom or utilized with reading groups during guided reading.

Process of *Jacob's Ladder*

The process of inquiry and feedback, as led and modeled by the teacher, is critical to the success of the program and student mastery of process skills. Teachers need to encourage and solicit multiple student responses and encourage dialogue about various perspectives and interpretations of a given text, requiring students to justify their answers with textual support and concrete examples. Student use of the ladders depends on teacher stance and modeling as well as student readiness. After teacher modeling, students should understand how to use the ladders as prescribed by the teacher. Sample follow-up questions such as those listed below can be used by the teacher and posted in the classroom to help guide student discussion.

- That's interesting; does anyone have a different idea?

- What in the story makes you say that?

- What do you think the author means by . . . ?

- What do you think are the implications or consequences to . . . ?

- Did anyone view that differently? How?

- Does anyone have a different point of view? Justify your answer.

- In the story I noticed that . . . Do you think that might have significance to the overall meaning?

- I heard someone say that he thought the poem (story) was about . . . What do you think? Justify your answer from the events of the story.

- Do you notice any key words that might be significant? Why?

- Do you notice any words that give you a mental picture? Do those words have significance? What might they symbolize?

- I agree with . . . because

- I had a different idea than . . . because

Grouping Students

Jacob's Ladder may be used in a number of different grouping patterns. The program should be introduced initially as a whole-group activity directed by the teacher with appropriate open-ended questions, feedback, and monitoring. After students have examined each type of ladder with teacher guidance, they should be encouraged to use the program by writing ideas independently, sharing with a partner, and then discussing the findings with a group. The dyad approach provides maximal opportunities for student discussion of the readings and collaborative decisions about the answers to questions posed. One purpose of the program is to solicit meaningful discussion of the text. Like-ability groups are recommended (Kulik & Kulik, 1992) for discussion.

Pre- and Postassessments and Grading

The pre- and postassessments included in Appendix A were designed as a diagnostic-prescriptive approach to guide program implementation prior to the implementation of *Jacob's Ladder*. The pretest should be administered, scored, and then used to guide student instruction and the selection of readings for varied ability groups. Both the pre- and postassessment, scoring rubric, and sample exemplars for each rubric category and level are included in Appendix A along with exemplars to guide scoring.

In both the pre- and postassessments, students read a short passage and respond to the four questions. Question 1 focuses on implications and consequences (Ladder A); Question 2 on generalization, theme, and concept (Ladders B and C); Question 3 on inference (Ladder C); and Question 4 on creative synthesis (Ladder D). By analyzing each question and scored response, teachers may wish to guide reading selections toward the appropriate ladders and stories based on student need.

Upon conclusion of the program or as a midpoint check, the posttest may be administered to compare the pretest results and to measure growth in students' responses. These pre/post results could be used as part of a student portfolio, in a parent-teacher conference, or documentation of curriculum effectiveness and student progress. The pre- and postassessments were piloted to ensure that both forms were equivalent in difficulty (α = .76) and that the interrater reliability of scorers was appropriate (α = .81).

Student Reflection, Feedback, and Record Keeping

Students may use an answer sheet such as the one provided in Appendix B for each ladder to record their personal thoughts independently before discussing with a partner. After finishing both of the ladders for each reading selection, a reflection page (also in Appendix B) can be provided, indicating the student's personal assessment of the work completed. Teachers also will want to check student answers as ladder segments are completed and conduct an error analysis. Individual or small-group consultation should occur at this time to ensure that students understand what they did incorrectly and why. In order to analyze student responses and progress across the program, teachers need to monitor student performance, using the student answer sheets to indicate appropriate completion of tasks. Specific comments about student work also are important to promote growth and understanding of content.

Record-keeping sheets for the class also are provided in Appendix B. On these forms, teachers record student progress on a 3-point scale: 2 (*applies skills very effectively*), 1 (*understands and applies skills*), or a 0 (*needs more practice with the given skill set*) across readings and ladder sets. This form can be used as part of a diagnostic-prescriptive approach to selecting reading materials and ladders based on student understanding or the need for more practice.

Sample Concluding Activities

Grading the ladders and responses are at the teacher's discretion. Teachers should not overemphasize the lower rungs in graded activities. Lower rungs are intended only as a vehicle to the higher level questions at the top of the ladder. Instead, top rung questions may be used as a journal prompt or as part of a graded open-ended writing response. Grades also could be given based on guided discussion after students are trained on appropriate ways to discuss literature. Additional ideas for grading are as follows:

- Write a persuasive essay to justify what you think the story is about.

- Create a symbol to show the meaning of the story. Write two sentences to justify your answer.

- In one word or phrase, what is this story mostly about? Justify your answer using examples from the story.
- Write a letter from the author's point of view, explaining what the meaning of the story is to young children.
- Pretend you are an illustrator. Create a drawing for the story or poem that shows the main idea or theme. Write a sentence that describes your illustration and theme.

Time Allotment

Although the time needed to complete *Jacob's Ladder* tasks will vary by student, most ladders should take students 15 minutes to read the selection and another 15–20 minutes to complete one ladder individually. More time is required for paired student and whole-group discussion of the questions. Teachers may wish to set aside 2 days each week for focusing on one *Jacob's Ladder* reading and the two commensurate ladders, especially when introducing the program.

Answer Key

An answer key is included at the end of the book. It contains a set of suggested answers for all questions related to each reading selection. All of the questions are somewhat open-ended; therefore, answers may vary. The answers provided in the key are simply suggestions to help illustrate the skills targeted by each ladder skill set.

Alignment to Standards

Tables 3, 4, and 5 contain alignment charts to demonstrate the connection of the fiction and nonfiction reading materials to relevant national standards in all subject areas. One of the benefits of this program is its ability to provide cross-disciplinary coverage of standards through the use of a single reading stimulus.

TABLE 3
Standards Alignment: Short Stories

Language Arts: Short Stories	The Ant and the Dove	The Crow and the Pitcher	Daedalus and Icarus	The Dog and His Reflection	The Fisherman and His Wife	The Judge	The Lion and the Gnat	The Mice in Council	The North Wind and the Sun	The Tap Dancer
The student will use analysis of text, including the interaction of the text with reader's feelings and attitudes, to create response.	✖	✖	✖	✖	✖	✖	✖	✖	✖	✖
The student will interpret and analyze the meaning of literary works from diverse cultures and authors by applying different critical lenses and analytic techniques.	✖	✖	✖	✖	✖	✖	✖	✖	✖	✖
The student will integrate various cues and strategies to comprehend what he or she reads.	✖	✖	✖	✖	✖	✖	✖	✖	✖	✖
The student will use a knowledge of the purposes, structures, and elements of writing to analyze and interpret various types of text.	✖	✖	✖	✖	✖	✖	✖	✖	✖	✖
Students will use word-analysis skills, context clues, and other strategies to read fiction and nonfiction with fluency and accuracy.	✖	✖	✖	✖	✖	✖	✖	✖	✖	✖

TABLE 4
Standards Alignment: Poetry

Language Arts: Poetry	Artist	City	Delilah	Fog	Imagination	Remembering	A Rose	Under My Bed	Windy Nights	Winter Horses
The student will use analysis of text, including the interaction of the text with reader's feelings and attitudes, to create response.	✗	✗		✗		✗	✗			✗
The student will interpret and analyze the meaning of literary works from diverse cultures and authors by applying different critical lenses and analytic techniques.		✗								
The student will integrate various cues and strategies to comprehend what he or she reads.	✗	✗	✗	✗	✗	✗	✗	✗	✗	✗
The student will use a knowledge of the purposes, structures, and elements of writing to analyze and interpret various types of text.	✗	✗	✗	✗	✗	✗	✗	✗	✗	✗
Students will use word-analysis skills, context clues, and other strategies to read fiction and nonfiction with fluency and accuracy.	✗	✗	✗	✗	✗	✗	✗	✗	✗	✗

TABLE 5
Standards Alignment: Nonfiction

Social Studies, Science, and Math Standards: Nonfiction	Ancient Rome	The Circle of Life	Geometry All Around Us	The Industrial Revolution	What's the Chance?	A World of Resources
Social Studies Standards						
Culture				✗		
Time, Continuity, and Change	✗			✗		
People, Places, and Environments				✗		
Individual Development and Identity						
Individuals, Groups, and Institutions	✗					
Science, Technology, and Society				✗		
Science Standards						
Science as Inquiry						
Physical Science						
Life Science		✗				
Earth and Space Science						✗
Science and Technology						
Science in Personal and Social Perspectives						
History and Nature of Science						
Math Standards						
Number and Operations					✗	
Geometry			✗			
Measurement						
Data Analysis and Probability					✗	
Problem Solving					✗	
Communication						
Connections						

References

American Federation of Teachers. (1998). *Building on the best, learning from what works: Seven promising reading and English language arts programs.* Washington, DC: Author.

Chin, C. A., Anderson, R. C., & Waggoner, M. A. (2001). Patterns of discourse in two kinds of literature discussion. *Reading Research Quarterly, 36,* 378–411.

Fielding, L. G., & Pearson, P. D. (1994). Reading comprehension: What works. *Educational Leadership, 51*(5), 62–67.

Guthrie, J. T., Schafer, W. D., & Huang, C. (2001). Benefits of opportunity to read and balanced reading instruction on the NAEP. *Journal of Educational Research, 94,* 145–162.

Knapp, M. S., Adelman, N. E., Marder, C., McCollum, H., Needels, M. C., Padilla, C., et al. (1995). *Teaching for meaning in high-poverty classrooms.* New York: Teachers College Press.

Kulik, J. A., & Kulik, C.-L. C. (1992). Meta-analytic findings on grouping programs. *Gifted Child Quarterly, 36,* 73–77.

Pressley, M., Wharton-McDonald, R., Allington, R., Block, C. C., Morrow, L., Tracey, D., et al. (2001). A study of effective first-grade literacy instruction. *Scientific Studies of Reading, 5,* 35–58.

Rawson, K. A., Dunlosky, J., & Thiede, K. W. (2000). The rereading effect: Metacomprehension accuracy improves across reading trials. *Memory & Cognition, 28,* 1004–1010.

Stambaugh, T. (2008). *Effects of the Jacob's Ladder Reading Comprehension Program.* Manuscript submitted for publication.

Taylor, B. M., Pearson, P. D., Peterson, D. S., & Rodriguez, M. C. (2003). Reading growth in high-poverty classrooms: The influence of teacher practices that encourage cognitive engagement in literacy learning. *The Elementary School Journal, 104,* 3–30.

Taylor, B. M., Peterson, D. S., Pearson, P. D., & Rodriguez, M. C. (2002). Looking inside classrooms: Reflecting on the "how" as well as the "what" in effective reading instruction. *Reading Teacher, 56,* 270–279.

Tivnan, T., & Hemphill, L. (2005). Comparing four literacy reform models in high-poverty schools: Patterns of first grade achievement. *Elementary School Journal, 105,* 419–443.

Villaume, S. K., & Brabham, E. G. (2002). Comprehension instruction: Beyond strategies. *The Reading Teacher, 55,* 672–676.

Part II:
Readings and Student Ladder Sets

Short Stories (Myths and Fables)

Chapter 1 includes the selected readings and accompanying question sets for each myth or fable selection. Each reading is followed by one or two sets of questions; each set is aligned to one of the four ladder skills.

For *Jacob's Ladder 1* the skills covered by each selection are as follows:

The Ant and the Dove
Originally told by Aesop

A thirsty ant crawled to the edge of the river to quench its thirst. The rapidly moving stream snatched the ant as it rushed by and almost drowned it. A white dove sitting on a tree plucked a leaf and let it fall into the stream close to him. The ant climbed on the leaf and floated to safety on the bank of the river. Not long after this event a hunter came and stood under the same tree from which the dove had watched the struggling ant. The hunter sighted the dove and drew his bow to pierce his target. The ant, perceiving his plan, stung him on his foot. The hunter cried out in pain and dropped his bow. The noise made the dove fly away.

Moral: One good turn deserves another.

A3

Consequences and Implications

What were the overall consequences of the Dove's actions?

Cause and Effect

A2

There are several cause and effect relationships in the fable. Complete the chart below, outlining causes and effects in the tale.

Cause	Effect

Sequencing

A1

List the events in the order they occur in the story.

THE ANT AND THE DOVE

Generalizations

B3

"One good turn deserves another" is a generalization about this fable.

- Write another generalization about the fable that you think is important.

Classifications

B2

What are the "good turns" that occur in the fable? Why is each a "good turn"? Fill in the following table.

Good Turn	Why?

Details

B1

What are some images you picture when you read this fable? Which phrases support those pictures? List at least four.

THE ANT AND THE DOVE

The Crow and the Pitcher

Originally told by Aesop

A crow, dying of thirst, came upon a pitcher that once had been full of water. When the crow put his beak into the mouth of the pitcher, he found that only very little water was left in it, and he could not reach far enough to get at it. He tried and tried, but at last had to give up in despair.

Then a thought came to him. He took a pebble and dropped it into the pitcher. Then he took another pebble and dropped it into the pitcher. Then he took another pebble and dropped it into the pitcher. Then he took another pebble and dropped it into the pitcher. Then he took another pebble and dropped it into the pitcher. At last he saw the water rising toward him, and after casting a few more pebbles into the pitcher, he was able to drink and save his life.

THE CROW AND THE PITCHER

Consequences and Implications

A3

What would have happened if the crow had done the following:
- Kept putting his beak in the pitcher?
- Flown away?
- Broken the pitcher?
- Waited for rain?

Cause and Effect

A2

What caused the water to reach the crow?
What overall effect did it have on the crow?

Sequencing

A1

What steps did the crow use to get water? List them below in order:

1. _____
2. _____
3. _____
4. _____

THE CROW AND THE PITCHER

Theme/Concept

C3

What main idea(s) did you get from this story?

Inference

C2

What made the crow successful in getting a drink of water?
Why did his plan work?

Literary Elements

C1

What are the crow's most important qualities? What other characters have you read about that show similar life qualities? How were their situations similar to or different from the crow's situation?

Daedalus and Icarus

Once upon a time in Ancient Greece, there was an architect by the name of Daedalus who loved his son and his work above all else. When the king of the island of Crete entrusted Daedalus with the job of designing and building his new palace, Daedalus was overjoyed and took his son, Icarus, to accompany him on the new project. He worked long and hard; the palace he built was nothing short of spectacular—the gardens were as beautiful as in a fairy tale; the living quarters were fit for a king; and there was an underground labyrinth that was supposed to be kept secret. The king inspected the finished project and loved it. Daedalus thought his job was through and started packing his and Icarus' belongings for the trip back home. The king, however, had other plans. If he was to ensure the labyrinth would be kept a secret, then he could not allow Daedalus and Icarus to leave! Trying to be nice, the king provided the architect and Icarus luxurious living space in the highest tower of the new palace, fine foods, even servants. None of it, however, could replace their freedom or their home.

Wise and patient, Daedalus started feeding wild birds on a windowsill. Every day as the birds ate, they shed a few feathers. After awhile, Daedalus had collected a lot of feathers and some leftover wax candles. As part of an escape plan, Daedalus fashioned two sets of wings with the feathers set in wax. Donning one, he gave the other set to his son, Icarus, but warned him: "Don't fly too low or the sea will soak your feathers. Don't fly too high or the sun will melt your wax."

Together they flew from their prison, up into the air. Icarus beat his arms and soared after his father. The sea shimmered below him. To fly, he thought! To soar with the gulls! He loved it. Icarus grew so excited by his new power, he flew upward toward the clouds, forgetting his father's warning.

Suddenly, a feather loosened from his artificial wings. Then another fell off. He stared at them. The wax was melting fast! His wings were coming apart! He had flown too close to the sun!

At this very moment Daedalus turned and could do nothing but watch helplessly as the wax melted from Icarus' wings, and Icarus plummeted to the unforgiving sea.

A3

Consequences and Implications

What implications might this myth have for your own life? For society?

A2

Cause and Effect

What was the effect of Icarus not heeding his father's warning and flying too close to the sun?

A1

Sequencing

List the events that occurred in this myth as you read them in the text (in order).

DAEDALUS AND ICARUS

C3

Theme/Concept

How is freedom a theme/main idea in this myth? Express your understanding by filling in as many bubbles as you can in the diagram below.

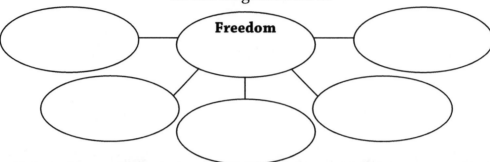

Freedom

C2

Inference

Why do you think Icarus did not obey his father's instructions?

C1

Literary Elements

List all of the characters in the myth and their relationships to each other. Use the chart below to help you.

Character	Relationship

What is the setting (place and time) of "Daedalus and Icarus?"

DAEDALUS AND ICARUS

The Dog and His Reflection
Originally told by Aesop

A dog, to whom the butcher had thrown a bone, was hurrying home with his prize as fast as he could go. As he crossed a narrow footbridge, he happened to look down and saw himself reflected in the quiet water as if in a mirror. But the greedy dog thought he saw a real dog carrying a bone much bigger than his own.

If he had stopped to think, he would have known better. But instead of thinking, he dropped his bone and sprang at the dog in the river, only to find himself swimming for dear life to reach the shore. At last he managed to scramble out, and as he stood sadly thinking about the good bone he had lost, he realized what a stupid dog he had been.

Moral: It is very foolish to be greedy.

Consequences and Implications

A3

- What "price" did the dog pay for his actions in the story?

- What did he lose? (Think of all of the possibilities!)

- What do you think he will do the next time he sees his reflection?

Cause and Effect

A2

- What *caused* the dog to lose his bone?

- What *effect* did it have on him?

- Draw a before and after cartoon picture of the dog and write a caption for each cartoon.

Sequencing

A1

Make a list of events in the story, beginning with what happens first, then second, and so forth.

THE DOG AND HIS REFLECTION

C3

Theme/Concept

What important ideas does the story tell us?

C2

Inference

What inference do you make from the sentence: "But the greedy dog thought he saw a real dog carrying a bone much bigger than his own"?

C1

Literary Elements

What qualities does the dog possess? Make a chart illustrating both the positive and negative aspects of each quality you identify.

Qualities	Positive	Negative

THE DOG AND HIS REFLECTION

The Fisherman and His Wife
By Jakob Grimm and Wilhelm Grimm

There once was a fisherman and his wife who lived together in a hut by the seashore. The fisherman went out every day with his hook and line to catch fish, and he angled and angled.

One day he was sitting with his rod, looking into the clear water, when suddenly down went the line to the bottom of the water. When he drew it up, he found a great fish on the hook.

The fish said to him, "Fisherman, listen to me. Let me go. I am not a real fish but an enchanted prince. What good shall I be to you if you land me? I shall not taste good. So put me back into the water again and let me swim away."

"Well," said the fisherman, "no need of so many words about the matter. As you can speak, I had much rather let you swim away." So he cast him back into the sea. Then the fisherman went home to his wife in the hut.

"Well, husband," said the wife, "have you caught anything today?"

"No," said the man. "That is, I did catch a huge fish, but as he said he was an enchanted prince, I let him go again."

"Did you not wish for something?" asked his wife.

"No," said the man. "What should I wish for?"

"Oh dear!" said the wife. "It is so dreadful always to live in this hut. You might as well have wished for a little cottage. I daresay he'd give it to us. Go and be quick."

When he went back, the sea was green and yellow and not nearly so clear. So he stood and said:

> Oh, man of the sea, come listen to me,
> For Alice, my wife, the plague of my life,
> Has sent me to ask a boon of thee.

Then the fish came swimming up and said, "Now then, what does she want?"

"Oh," said the man, "my wife says that I should have asked you for something when I caught you. She does not want to live any longer in the hut and would rather have a cottage."

"Go home," said the fish. "She has it already."

So the man went home and found, instead of the hut, a little cottage, and his wife was sitting on a bench before the door. She took him by the hand and said to him, "Come in and see if this is not a great deal better." They went in, and there was a little sitting room and a beautiful little bedroom, a kitchen and a larder, with all sorts of furniture, and iron and brassware of the very best. And, at the back was a little yard with chickens and ducks, and a little garden full of green vegetables and fruit.

"Look," said the wife, "is not that nice?"

"Yes," said the man. "If this can only last, we shall be happy the rest of our days."

"We will see about that," said his wife.

All went well for a week or fortnight. Then the wife said, "Look here, husband, the cottage is really too small. I think the fish had better give us a larger house. I should like very much to live in a large stone castle. So go to your fish, and he will send us a castle."

"Oh, my dear wife!" said the man. "The cottage is good enough. What do we want a castle for?"

"Go along," said the wife. "He might just as well give it to us as not. Do as I say."

The man did not want to go, and he said to himself, "It is not the right thing to do."

Nevertheless he went. When he came to the seaside, the water was purple and dark blue and gray and dark, and not green and yellow as before. And he stood and said:

> Oh, man of the sea, come listen to me,
> For Alice, my wife, the plague of my life,
> Has sent me to ask a boon of thee.

"Now then, what does she want?" asked the fish.

"Oh!" said the man, half-frightened. "She wants to live in a large stone castle."

"Go home. She is already standing before the door," said the fish.

Then the man went home, as he supposed. But when he arrived, there stood in the place of the cottage a great castle of stone, and his wife was standing on the steps about to go in. So she took him by the hand and said, "Let us enter."

With that he went in with her. In the castle was a great hall with a marble floor, and there were a great many servants, who led them through the large door. The passages were decked with tapestry and the rooms with golden chairs and tables. Crystal chandeliers were hanging from the ceiling, and all the rooms had carpets. The tables were spread with the most delicious foods for anyone who wanted them. At the back of the house was a stable yard for horses and cattle and carriages of the finest. Besides, there was a splendid large garden with the most beautiful flowers and fine fruit trees, and also a park, for half a mile long, with deer, oxen, sheep, and everything the heart could wish for.

"There," said the wife, "is not this beautiful?"

"Oh, yes," said the man. "If it will only last, we can live in this fine castle and be very well contented."

"We will see about that," said the wife.

The next morning the wife awakened at the break of day, and she looked out of her window and saw the beautiful country lying all around.

"Husband," she called, "look out of the window. Just think if we could be King over all this country. Go to your fish and tell him we should like to be King."

"Now, wife," said the man. "What should we be Kings for? I don't want to be King."

"Well," said the wife, "if you don't want to be King, I will be. You must go at once to the fish. I must be King."

So the man went, very much put out that his wife should want to be King. He did not at all want to go, and yet he went all the same.

When he came to the sea, the water was dark and gray and rushed far inland, and he stood there and said:

> Oh, man of the sea, come listen to me,
> For Alice, my wife, the plague of my life,
> Has sent me to ask a boon of thee.

"Now then, what does she want?" asked the fish.

"Oh, dear!" said the man. "She wants to be King."

"Go home. She is so already," said the fish.

So the man went back, and as he came to the palace, he saw it was very much larger and had great towers and splendid gateways. The herald stood before the door, and there were a number of soldiers with kettledrums and trumpets.

When he came inside, everything was of marble and gold, and there were many curtains with great gold tassels. Then he went through the doors to the throne room, and there was his wife, sitting upon a throne of gold and diamonds, and she had a great golden crown on her head, and the scepter in her hand was of pure gold and jewels, and on each side stood six pages in a row, each one a head shorter than the other. So the man went up to her and said, "Well, wife, so now you are King."

"Yes," said she. "Now I am King."

Then he stood and looked at her, and when he had gazed at her for some time he said, "Well, wife, this is fine for you to be King. Now there is nothing more to ask for."

"Oh, husband!" said the wife, seeming quite restless. "I am tired of this already. Go to your fish and tell him that now I am King, I must be Emperor."

"Now, wife," said the man, "what do you want to be Emperor for?"

"Husband," said she, "go and tell the fish I want to be Emperor."

"Oh, dear!" said the man. "He could not do it. I cannot ask him such a thing. There is but one Emperor at a time. The fish can't possibly make anyone Emperor—indeed he can't."

"Now, look here," said the wife, "I am King, and you are only my husband, so will you go at once? Go along. For if he was able to make me King he is able to make me Emperor, and I will and must be Emperor. So go along."

So he was obliged to go. And as he went he felt very uncomfortable about it, and he thought to himself, "It is not at all the right thing to do. To want to be Emperor is going too far; the fish will soon get tired of this."

With this he came to the sea, and the water was quite black, and the foam flew, and the wind blew, and the man was terrified. But he stood and said:

Oh, man of the sea, come listen to me,
For Alice, my wife, the plague of my life,
Has sent me to ask a boon of thee.

"What is it now?" asked the fish.

"Oh, dear!" said the man. "My wife wants to be Emperor."

"Go home," said the fish. "She is Emperor already."

So the man went home and found the castle adorned with polished marble and golden gates. The troops were being marshaled before the door, and they were blowing trumpets and beating drums. And when he entered he saw barons, earls, and dukes waiting about like servants, and the doors were of bright gold. He saw his wife sitting upon a throne of solid gold, and it was about 2 miles high. She had a great golden crown on, set in precious stones, and in one hand she had a scepter, and in the other a globe; and on both sides of her stood pages in two rows, all arranged according to size, from the enormous giant of 2 miles high, to the tiniest dwarf the size of my little finger, and before her stood earls and dukes in crowds.

So the man went up to her and said, "Well, wife, so now you are Emperor. I hope you are contented at last."

"We will see about that," said his wife.

With that they went to bed. But she was as far as ever from being contented, and she could not get to sleep for thinking of what she would like to be next.

The next morning as she sat before the window watching the sun rise, she said, "Oh, I have it! What if I should make the sun and moon to rise? Husband," she called, "wake up and go to your fish and tell him I want power over the sun and moon."

"Oh, wife!" said the man. "The fish cannot do that. Do be contented, I beg of you."

But she became most impatient and said, "I can wait no longer. Go at once."

So off he went, as well as he could for fright. And a dreadful storm arose, so that he could hardly keep on his feet. The houses and trees were blown down, and the mountains trembled, and rocks fell in the sea. The sky was quite black; and it thundered and lightning flashed; and the waves, crowned with foam, ran mountains high. So he cried out:

> Oh, man of the sea, come listen to me,
> For Alice, my wife, the plague of my life,
> Has sent me to ask a boon of thee.

"Well, what now?" said the fish.

"Oh, dear!" said the man. "She wants to order about the sun and the moon."

"Go home with you," said the fish, "And you will find her And there they are sitting to this very day.

A3

Consequences and Implications

What were the consequences for the wife of her continued demands on the enchanted fish?

A2

Cause and Effect

What effect did the husband's continued willingness to take his wife's demands to the fish have on his wife's actions?

A1

Sequencing

The following events from the story are not in order. How would you sequence them to tell the story?

- The wife wanted to be emperor.
- The fisherman caught an enchanted fish.
- The wife wanted a cottage.
- The wife told the fisherman he should have asked the fish to grant him a wish.
- The sea was black and the wind was blowing.
- The wife was returned to the hut in which she and the fisherman originally lived.
- The sea was green and yellow.

THE FISHERMAN AND HIS WIFE

The Judge: A Tale From West Africa

From Touchpebbles

Two mice stole a large chunk of cheese. Both wanted to have what they thought was their fair share. But neither of them trusted the other to divide the cheese fairly. So they went to the lion, the king of all animals. "King, we want to divide this cheese, but we can't do it fairly. We can't agree on what is fair. Please help us." The lion frowned at the mice because he was very busy but believed it was his duty to help. "I'll send you to the monkey. He's the judge and will help you, but it would be better if you could do it yourselves. Once you bring in a judge, many new problems might come up." But the mice wanted the monkey, and so the king sent them to his law court.

The monkey was seated in a big chair behind a large table. The mice asked for his help in dividing the cheese. The monkey said, "Of course I'll be the judge if you want me to." He sent his helper for a scale and a knife. With the knife, he cut the cheese so that one piece was much bigger than the other. Then he ate some of the bigger piece. The mice asked him what he was doing. "I'm eating from this piece so that it will be equal to the smaller piece," he said. He ate so much that when he put both pieces on the scale again, the one that used to be smaller was now bigger. So he began to eat from that piece. The mice now realized that the monkey planned to eat all the cheese. They said, "Give us what's left, O Judge, and we will divide it fairly." But the monkey said, "No. You will fight each other and then King Lion will be angry with me." So the monkey went on eating until all of the cheese was gone. Then one mouse turned to the other and said, "Why didn't we trust each other and cut the cheese ourselves?"

Consequences and Implications

A3

Why did the lion try to warn the mice about asking the monkey for help? How do you know?

What is the moral of the story? Support your answer.

Cause and Effect

A2

What did the lion say would happen if the mice went to the monkey for help with dividing the cheese?

What happened after the monkey ate part of the larger piece of cheese? What was the final outcome of the monkey's solution to the mice's problem?

Sequencing

A1

To whom did the mice go to for help first? Second?

The following actions taken by the monkey are not in order. How would you sequence them to tell the story correctly?
- He ate the largest piece of cheese.
- He told the mice they would fight and the King would be angry.
- He ate all the cheese.
- He agreed to help the mice.
- He weighed the cheese again.

THE JUDGE: A TALE FROM WEST AFRICA

The Lion and the Gnat

Originally told by Aesop

A lion was enraged by a gnat that was buzzing around his head, but the gnat was not the least disturbed. "Do you think," he said spitefully, "that I am afraid of you because they call you king?" Then he flew at the lion and stung him sharply on the nose. In fury the lion struck at the gnat, but only succeeded in tearing himself with his claws. Again and again the gnat stung the lion, who was now roaring terribly. At last, worn out with rage and covered with wounds made by his own teeth and claws, the lion gave up the fight. The gnat buzzed away to tell the whole world about his victory, but instead flew straight into a spider's web. There, he who had defeated the king of beasts came to a miserable end, the prey of a little spider.

THE LION AND THE GNAT

Consequences and Implications

A3

What do you see as consequences of the following situations in life:
- Being smaller than other creatures?
- Being larger than other creatures?
- Being too clever?
- Being too proud?

Cause and Effect

A2

What caused the gnat to get caught? What effect did it have on him?

Sequencing

A1

Draw three scenes in sequence that depict the main events that happened in this story. Title each scene.

C3

Theme/Concept

What major ideas does the story tell us? Write a story with human characters that is similar to this animal story.

C2

Inference

What evidence is there in the story that the gnat was proud? Why did he feel this way?

C1

Literary Elements

The main characters are a lion and a gnat. Complete a comparison chart to show how different they are.

Characters	Similarities	Differences
Lion		
Gnat		

THE LION AND THE GNAT

The Mice in Council
Originally told by Aesop

Once upon a time, the mice, feeling constantly in danger from a cat, called a meeting to decide upon the best means of getting rid of this continual annoyance. Many plans were discussed and rejected. At last, a young mouse got up and proposed that a bell should be hung around the cat's neck, so that from then on they would always have advanced warning of her coming, and so be able to escape. This suggestion was hailed with the greatest applause and unanimous agreement. Upon which an old mouse, who had sat silent all the while, got up and said that he considered the plan most clever, and that it would, no doubt, solve their problem. But he had one question to ask: Which one of them was going to put the bell around the cat's neck?

Consequences and Implications

A3

What implication might you make about "age and experience" based on the story?

Cause and Effect

A2

Complete the following chart:

In the story, the cat *caused*:	The *effect* was that the mice:

Sequencing

A1

Describe, in order, four steps the mice might take to put the bell on the cat.

THE MICE IN COUNCIL

THE MICE IN COUNCIL

Theme/Concept

C3

What main ideas does the story teach us about groups? About how to solve problems?

Inference

C2

What inference do you draw from the last sentence: "Which one of them was going to put the bell around the cat's neck?" What does it mean?

Literary Elements

C1

Why are cats and mice natural enemies? List qualities and habits of each in the following chart:

	Qualities	**Habits**
Cats		
Mice		

The North Wind and the Sun
Originally told by Aesop

Over a period of time, the wind and the sun quarreled with one another. The wind, having great power and strong force, was convinced that he was stronger than the sun. He looked for every opportunity to prove his position. The sun, confident in her intense heat and awesome light, was sure that her powers were much greater than the powers or force of the wind.

It just so happened, on a particular day, a lone traveler was walking down a long, dusty road. The sun approached the wind and said: "I have a plan that will settle our quarrel as to which of us is the stronger." The wind stared at the sun in disbelief. What plan had the sun now concocted to prove she was the stronger?

The sun revealed her plan to the wind. "I believe that whichever one of us can cause that lone traveler to take off his coat shall be declared to be the stronger. In fact, I want to be very fair in this task, so I will let you go first."

The sun made her way behind a large black cloud, at which point the wind began to blow as hard as he could blow. He blew directly on the traveler, until the traveler wrapped his coat more closely around his body. No matter how hard the wind blew, it was in vain. The man only clung more tightly to his coat. Finally, in despair, the wind had to give up.

Coming out from behind the huge black cloud, the sun shone brightly with all of her intensity upon the weary traveler. The traveler, beginning to perspire from the heat of the direct sun, found it too hot to continue without relief. At this point he stopped and took off his coat and continued on with his journey.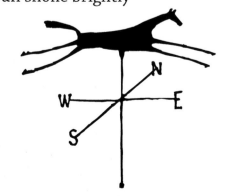

Moral: It is easier to use persuasion than try to win with force.

A3

Consequences and Implications

Think about the two ways the sun and the wind tried to influence the traveler. Why do you think the sun's method was more effective?

Could the wind have done anything differently?

A2

Cause and Effect

What was the effect of the wind blowing forcefully on the traveler?

A1

Sequencing

What happened when the young wind blew the first time?
The second time?

THE NORTH WIND AND THE SUN

Generalizations

B3

What generalizations can you make about the relationship of power and persuasion?

Classifications

B2

Create two columns. In column one, list times when you have seen or read about persuasion being more powerful than force. In column two, list times you have seen or read about power winning over persuasion.

Details

B1

What was the strength of the wind?

What was the strength of the sun?

Which was stronger and why?

THE NORTH WIND AND THE SUN

The Tap Dancer
Author Unknown

There once was a horse who dreamed of becoming a famous tap dancer. He loved dancing more than anything. He found a flat concrete section near a riverbank where he could practice his dance steps. Every day the horse would practice on the concrete, his hooves hitting the solid ground, making wonderful tapping sounds.

After much practice the horse said, "I am now a tap dancer." He held a recital so that all of his friends could watch him dance. All of his animal friends came to watch the performance. The horse gave a wonderful show, giving his best effort. When the horse was done, he took a deep bow.

There was silence. Not one of his friends clapped for the horse and his tap dancing. One friend said, "You're not a tap dancer. You are only a horse, an animal just like us. You will never be a dancer." All of the other animals laughed as they walked away, leaving the horse alone.

The horse said to himself, "I am a great dancer. I know it. I will continue to dance for myself." And so he did! He enjoyed many years of tap dancing on the riverbank. Even though his friends did not understand his dream, he continued to dance for himself!

Consequences and Implications

A3

What would have happened if the audience had clapped?
How would it have changed the outcome of the story?

Cause and Effect

A2

What *effect* did his friends' laughter have on the horse? Think of a time someone has laughed at you. How was your reaction similar or different from that of the horse in the story?

Sequencing

A1

List the *three* most important events from the story in order.

THE TAP DANCER

Theme/Concept

C3

What important idea does the story of "The Tap Dancer" tell us?

Inference

C2

What evidence or details in the story tell you that the horse was serious about becoming a great tap dancer?

Literary Elements

C1

What character traits does the horse possess?
What do you admire about him?

THE TAP DANCER

CHAPTER 2

Poetry

Chapter 2 includes the selected readings and accompanying question sets for each poetry selection. Each reading is followed by one or two sets of questions; each set is aligned to one of the four ladder skills.

For *Jacob's Ladder 1* the skills covered by each selection are as follows:

Title . . . . Ladder Skills

Artist C

City C

Delilah C

Fog . . . . B

Imagination . . . . B

Remembering C

A Rose . . . . A

Under My Bed . . . . B

Windy Nights . . . . A

Winter Horses C

Artist

The sun slants through the branches
colouring the leaves.
Soon the cold will come.
The leaves will fall.
Then,
the sun will be angry.
It can't paint anymore.

By Caitlin Graham
Grades 6–8
Honorable Mention
Center for Gifted Education Talent Search

Theme/Concept

C3

You have just read a poem about nature. What ideas do you think this poem is trying to tell us about nature?

Inference

C2

What do you infer is the reason the sun cannot paint anymore?

ARTIST

Literary Elements

C1

The character of the sun is given the role of artist in the poet's depiction of nature. Write a poem using another facet of nature as a person.

OR

How is the sun like an artist in the poem? **AND**

Draw what the first two lines of the poem would look like.

City

By Langston Hughes

In the morning the city
Spreads its wings
Making a song
In stone that sings.

In the evening the city
Goes to bed
Hanging lights
About its head.

Theme/Concept

C3

How does the title give the reader a clue about the main idea of the poem? Explain your answer using words from the poem.

Inference

C2

"In the evening the city / goes to bed / hanging lights / about its head."

What does the author mean by these lines? What can be inferred?

Select which answer below best describes the quote. Explain your answer using phrases from the poem.

- It is a starry night.
- It is dark except for the streetlights.
- The author wants to sleep with a nightlight above his head.
- There are always lights on in the city.

Literary Elements

C1

- Make a list of phrases or words that describe the city.
- How does the author use those words and phrases to put a picture in your head? What do you "see"? Why?
- Illustrate your vision of the poem based on the descriptive language used.

CITY

Delilah

She has blue eyes like the ocean.
Her tongue like a rose.
Her nose like a heart.
Her tail like a fan.
Her black coat like the night sky.

By Casey Carroll
Grades 4–5
Honorable Mention
Center for Gifted Education Talent Search

Theme/Concept

C3

Write a poem like "Delilah" to describe your pet or an animal you know.
(Use the poem as your model.)

Inference

C2

What evidence is important in deciding on Delilah's identity?

What or who is Delilah in the poem, based on the evidence?

DELILAH

Literary Elements

C1

What words does the poet use to show Delilah as a lovable creature?

Fog

By Carl Sandburg

The fog comes
On little cat feet.

It sits looking
Over harbor and city
On silent haunches
And then moves on.

B3

Generalizations

Can you create a poem that is like this one? Choose one natural element and one animal from the following table to help you.

Natural Elements	Animal
Sun	Dog
Fire	Horse
Wind	Bird
Rain	Fish

Classifications

FOG

B2

The author chooses a cat to describe the fog. What characteristics of cats might have made the author choose it? Make a list of these cat characteristics.

Details

B1

Draw a picture that might go along with the poem. Write a sentence to explain your picture.

Name: _____ Date: _____

Imagination

Anything is possible
As you can plainly see
Fish are flying in the sky
And birds are in the sea

Dogs are walking people
And cats are walking dogs
A shark is soundly sleeping
While turtles play with frogs

Panda bears in Canada
And Kangaroos in boots
Chameleons run around and hide
In their tiny suits

If you use your imagination
There is nothing you can't do
If you want to write a poem
Express yourself and be you!

By Graham Walsh
Grades 4–5
Third Place
Center for Gifted Education Talent Search

Generalizations

Generalizations are broad ideas that can apply to many situations. Write at least four generalizations you can make about funny images based on the poem and your list and your categories from Questions B2 and B1. You may use the chart below to help organize your ideas.

B3

Generalization	Evidence From the Poem	Evidence From My List

Classifications

B2

Using your list from Question 2 in Section B1, develop categories for your funny images. Put each image into a category. How are your categories similar? How are they different?

Details

B1

"Imagination" is a very funny poem. What details in the poem make it funny? Draw a picture of at least one funny image from the poem.

Brainstorm a list of funny images (like the ones in "Imagination"). Write down at least 25.

IMAGINATION

Remembering

A small brown cottage stands by a lake
Lonely, abandoned, and sad,
One time filled with children, laughter, and song,
It sighs for the life it once had.

It looks out o'er the forest, so old,
And the lake, deserted and chilled,
And the overgrown garden once cared for and loved,
Which one time with roses was filled.

It gazes down the sleeping road,
Wending its way into the night,
It stares up at the dusky, darkening sky,
Where the stars shed their twinkling light.

Even the moon, so pale and austere,
Looks down tenderly from above,
And the small brown cottage will stand forever,
Thinking back on the days of love.

By Emily Howell
Grades 4–5
First Place
Center for Gifted Education Talent Search

Theme/Concept

C3

Change can be positive or negative. Is the change the house experienced positive or negative? How do you know? What other ideas does the poem convey besides change?

Inference

C2

Why do you think the house feels sad and lonely? What line(s) from the poem support your inference?

Do you think the house would prefer to return to the "days of love"? Why or why not? Use lines from the poem to support your inference.

Literary Elements

C1

Personification is a literary term used when writers give human characteristics to objects. Does the cottage demonstrate human qualities? If so, how? Use text from the poem to support your answer.

REMEMBERING

A Rose

A rose grows every day,
In a land of grass and hay.
All alone and with a cold,
The old rose grows old.
Its leaves start to curl and crisp,
And crunch into a dust-like mist.
As it falls to the dirt,
The old rose feels very hurt.
But when spring comes to face,
A new rose comes to take its place.

By Emma Tisdale
Grades 4–5
Second Place
Center for Gifted Education Talent Search

Consequences and Implications

A3

What if the seasons never changed? What would be the consequences for the rose if it was always summer? If it was always winter? What would be the consequences for people if it was always summer? If it was always winter?

What does the poem imply about the natural cycle of living things? Support your answer.

Cause and Effect

A2

A ROSE

In "A Rose," the poet uses personification to give the rose human-like qualities. In line 8, the poet writes, "The old rose feels very hurt." What is the cause of the rose's pain? Is this pain physical or emotional? How do you know? Use lines from the poem to support your answer.

At the end of the poem, a new rose has come to take the place of the old rose. In your opinion, what effect does the growth of this new rose have?

Sequencing

A1

The cycle of the four seasons is an important part of this poem. In what season does the poem begin? In what season does it end? Create and illustrate a timeline of the poem, making sure to sequence the events in the correct order.

Under My Bed

From under my bed,
Where I lay my head,
Creep funny things,
And objects with wings.

From under my bed,
A ribbon of red,
Forms a road,
On which along hops a star-speckled toad.

From under my bed,
A picture is read,
Telling the story of a wind,
Dancing away from the cloud to which it was pinned.

From under my bed,
A tree darts ahead
In a race
With the rain's fast and musical pace.

From under my bed,
Dreams are typed; not to be said.
The mountains are soldiers at attention,
Waiting patiently to receive their pension.

Under my bed,
There lives a whole other world that came from my head,
Contained in that cramped space, which many dread,
Under my bed.

By Sarah Murphy
Grades 6–8
Second Place
Center for Gifted Education Talent Search

Generalizations

B3

Which word or phrase best explains the poem: (a) freedom of expression, (b) creativity, or (c) passion? Why? Use words from the poem to explain your answer.

Classifications

B2

The author uses many metaphors[1] in the poem. Make a list of each and comment on how each is used by the poet to convey her ideas.

[1] A metaphor is a direct comparison between two objects, without using "like" or "as." Example: My bed is a ship that sails me away.

Details

B1

Two students were arguing about what the poem meant. One student said it was about a kid who didn't clean his room and had things growing under his bed. Another student said the poem was about someone who crawled under his bed to write and make up stories. Which student do you believe is correct? Make a list of words or phrases in the poem that help you know.

UNDER MY BED

Windy Nights

By Robert Louis Stevenson

Whenever the moon and stars are set,
Whenever the wind is high,
All night long in the dark and wet,
A man goes riding by.
Late in the night when the fires are out,
Why does he gallop and gallop about?

Whenever the trees are crying aloud,
And ships are tossed at sea,
By, on the highway, low and loud,
By at the gallop he goes, and then
By he comes back at the gallop again.

Consequences and Implications

A3

Who is "he" in the poem?
What clues do you have that might imply who "he" is?

Cause and Effect

A2

Wind causes many things to happen. What happens in the poem as a result of wind? Can you think of other effects that the wind causes?

Sequencing

A1

Which words does the author use multiple times? Do you think those are important to the order of the poem? Why or why not?

WINDY NIGHTS

Winter Horses

The clouds stir.
A storm approaches
like a band of wild colts.
Their twisted tails and
flying forelegs are
oak leaves dancing in the breeze.
Their shaking manes and flashing heels are just
snowflakes laughing at the wind.
Their defiant whinnies are
only the trees shuddering against the cold.
The frost that clings to the grass is the
lingering dust of their passage.

By Caitlin Graham
Grades 6–8
Honorable Mention
Center for Gifted Education Talent Search

C3

Theme/Concept

Select an animal to represent another season. Describe the qualities of the animal and the season in the chart below.

Animal	Season

Create a poem that compares the two, using "Winter Horses" as a model.

Title your poem so that it reflects a central idea.

C2

Inference

What evidence from the poem suggests that winter is only temporary?

C1

Literary Elements

Find the simile in the poem.

Identify the four metaphors in the poem.

WINTER HORSES

CHAPTER
3

Nonfiction

Chapter 3 includes the selected readings and accompanying question sets for each nonfiction selection. Each reading is followed by one or two sets of questions; each set is aligned to one of the four ladder skills.

For *Jacob's Ladder 1,* the skills covered by each selection are as follows:

Ancient Rome

According to legend, Rome was founded by twin brothers, Romulus and Remus, in 753 B.C. Archaeological evidence of Ancient Rome dates to the 8th century B.C., somewhere between 800 B.C. and 701 B.C. (Remember, in B.C., the smaller the number, the more recent the date, so 701 B.C. is closer to modern day than 800 B.C.) For nearly 1,000 years, Rome was the most important, richest, most powerful city in the Western world. During this time, Rome went through several major changes.

Rome began as the Roman Kingdom. It was ruled by a succession of seven kings. Some time between 509 B.C. and 501 B.C., the last of the seven kings, Tarquin the Proud, was deposed of his throne, which means he was removed from power. With the end of Tarquin the Proud's reign, the Roman Kingdom became the Roman Republic.

The Roman Republic was governed by a senate rather than a monarch or king. The original senate consisted of 100 heads of Roman families. The senate did not have actual lawmaking powers. Rather, it made recommendations to the Plebeian Council, which received its power from the Roman people. Over time, the senate grew in number and in power. By the end of the Roman Republic, there were more than 300 members of the senate. Although they did not have the power to make laws, the senate held remarkable political power. The senate was responsible for sending and receiving ambassadors to foreign lands, appointing managers of public lands, conducting wars, and distributing public funds.

The Roman Republic came to an end when, in the middle of the 1st century B.C., three men formed the First Triumvirate (trahy-**uhm**-ver-it). These three men were Julius Caesar, Pompey (**pom**-pee), and Crassus (**kras**-*uhs*). They plotted to control the Roman Republic and began a civil war. In 44 B.C., Julius Caesar was assassinated, or killed, by senators who did not agree with his politics. Eventually, through a series of struggles for power, Augustus, Caesar's designated heir, gained control and became the undisputed ruler of Rome.

With the ascent of Augustus to power in 31 B.C., the Roman Republic became the Roman Empire. The Roman Empire extended across most of Europe to the Mediterranean Sea with a population that exceeded 1 million people. During the "Reign of Five Good Emperors" from 96–180 A.D., the Roman Empire reached its largest land mass of 2.5 million square miles. Eventually, the Empire became so large that it was nearly impossible for one ruler to maintain control of the entire Empire. In 293 A.D., the Emperor Diocletian (dahy-*uh*-**klee**-shu*h*n) divided the Roman Empire into an eastern half and a western half. This division became permanent in 395 A.D. after Constantine established Constantinople as the capital of the Eastern

Roman Empire, which later became known as the Byzantine Empire. The Western Empire continued to be known as the Roman Empire. This Roman Empire came to a dramatic end in 410 A.D. when the Visigoths, an Eastern Germanic tribe, raided and sacked the city of Rome. The Byzantine Empire came to a less dramatic end in 1453 A.D. when the ruler of the Ottoman Empire, Mehmet II, conquered Constantinople.

Consequences and Implications

A3

What consequences did the Roman Empire experience because of its large size? What were the implications of these consequences? Justify your answer.

Cause and Effect

A2

What caused the Roman Republic to end? Use evidence from the text to support your answer.

Sequencing

A1

Create a timeline of the major events in the history of Ancient Rome.

ANCIENT ROME

ANCIENT ROME

Creative Synthesis

D3

Choose an era from Ancient Rome—the Roman Kingdom, the Roman Republic, or the Roman Empire. Imagine you are a Roman citizen during one of these eras. Write a journal entry about what is happening in your city.

Summarizing

D2

In three sentences or less, summarize the fall of the Roman Republic and the rise of the Roman Empire.

Paraphrasing

D1

Rewrite the following statement in your own words:

"For nearly 1,000 years, Rome was the most important, richest, most powerful city in the Western world."

The Circle of Life

All animals journey through a predictable life cycle during their lifespan. Most animals, except mammals that give birth to live young, begin as eggs. The female of the species lays the eggs, which begins the life cycle of a new animal. Different kinds of animals experience different life cycles. Let's compare the life cycle of amphibians (ām-fĭb'ē-ənz) and insects.

Amphibians

Amphibians, such as frogs, live their entire lives near water because they must return to the water to lay their eggs. Amphibians experience a three-stage life cycle. The stages are the egg stage, the larval stage, and the adult stage. The female amphibians lay their eggs directly in the water, thus beginning the egg stage. When the eggs hatch, the larval stage begins as tadpoles emerge with gills for breathing. As amphibians mature, they develop lungs that allow them to breathe outside of the water. They also begin growing legs and losing their tails. This process is called metamorphosis (met-*uh*-**mawr**-*fuh*-sis), which means a complete change in form. During metamorphosis, amphibians change from gill breathers to lung breathers and from plant eaters to meat eaters (think about a frog sitting on the side of pond catching bugs—meat—with its long, sticky tongue). Some amphibians, such as salamanders and newts, do not undergo metamorphosis. Instead, they spend their entire lives in the larval stage. They do not develop lungs or lose their tails, and they only grow very short legs.

Insects

Winged insects and nonwinged insects experience two different life cycles. Both types of insects begin as eggs. They both have a larval stage, a pupa stage, and a metamorphosis. However, they journey through these stages in different ways.

Nonwinged Insects

Nonwinged insects have a hard outer skeleton called an *exoskeleton* that protects them. Because of this hard outer covering, these insects must grow in stages. The insects eat, grow larger, and then must periodically shed their exoskeleton through a process called *ecdysis* (**ek**-*duh*-sis). Each time the insect sheds its exoskeleton, it is bigger and more mature. Therefore, metamorphosis—or the complete change from larvae to adult insect—happens gradually over time. Scientists have named this gradual change "simple metamorphosis."

Winged Insects

Winged insects, such as butterflies and ladybugs, experience four distinct life cycle phases. Like most other animals, they begin their lives as eggs. When they hatch, they enter the larval stage. During the larval stage, a butterfly is called a caterpillar and a ladybug is called a Lady Bird beetle. The length of the larval stage varies among species, but during this stage the insects eat and grow. Eventually, the larvae are ready to enter the next stage: The larvae become pupae by encasing themselves inside a chrysalis (**kris**-*uh*-lis) or cocoon. While in the chrysalis, the winged insect undergoes a complete transformation and emerges as an adult butterfly or ladybug. The adult winged insect looks completely different than the larva. Scientists have named this complete transformation *complex metamorphosis*.

Consequences and Implications

A3

What are the implications of an amphibian or an insect reaching the final stage in the life cycle?

Cause and Effect

A2

What causes a nonwinged insect to move to the next stage of simple metamorphosis?

Sequencing

A1

List, in order, the following:
- Stages of an amphibian's life cycle
- Stages of a winged insect's life cycle

THE CIRCLE OF LIFE

Creative Synthesis

D3

Write about the process of metamorphosis from the perspective of an amphibian, a nonwinged insect, or a winged insect.

Summarizing

D2

Describe the life cycle of nonwinged insects versus that of winged insects in three sentences or less.

Paraphrasing

D1

Rewrite this statement in your own words:

"Therefore, metamorphosis—or the complete change from larvae to adult insect—happens gradually over time. Scientists have named this gradual change *simple metamorphosis*."

THE CIRCLE OF LIFE

Geometry All Around Us

Have you ever looked around your classroom, your kitchen, or your backyard and noticed all of the geometry around you? Geometry includes all of the many shapes, lines, angles, points, quadrants, square inches, square feet, and square yards that you see every day.

Look around your classroom. How many different shapes can you find? The chalkboard at the front of the room is probably a rectangle. Perhaps the table where you sit is a circle. Maybe there is a globe somewhere in your classroom: A globe is a three-dimensional shape called a *sphere*. What about angles? How many angles do you see in your classroom? Perhaps your chair is connected to your desk. Is the seat at a 90-degree, or right, angle? Or, is it slightly tilted back at a 105- or 110-degree angle? Are the corners of the windows right angles?

Now let's think about your house. Your roof may be shaped like a triangle or perhaps a trapezoid. The walls in your house may form straight lines or they may have some angled corners. Do you know how many square feet are in your house? The architect who designed your house and the contractor who built it used geometry to determine how large each room should be, where the exterior and interior walls should go, and how much square footage the finished home should have. Can you think of another way geometry is used in the building of house? Here's one example: An architect creates a two-dimensional drawing of a house using lines, points, and angles. The architect gives this two-dimensional drawing to the contractor who then transforms it into a three-dimensional building.

Let's think about your yard. Are there flower gardens? How do your parents know how much potting soil or mulch to buy for the

flower gardens? They use geometry to figure out the areas of the different flowerbeds. Once they know the square footage of each bed, they know how much dirt or mulch is needed to fill each area. Farmers use this same technique when they are deciding how and where to plant their crops.

They use geometry to calculate the area of their fields. In places as large as fields, the area often is referred to as acres. One acre is 4,840 square yards or 43,560 square feet. That's a lot of area!

Geometry also is a big part of activities we do every day. For example, when you are driving somewhere new, how do you know where to go? You might look at a map. When looking at a map, you are using geometry. Maps are made up of quadrants, points, and lines. You use the map's key to determine in what quadrant your desired location is, then you follow the lines, or roads, until you reach your destination, which is a point on the map.

Have you ever ridden a skateboard or seen skateboarders riding on ramps? The skateboarders use geometry, even if they don't realize it, when they build their ramps. They must determine the perfect arc for the performance of their tricks. If the arc of the ramp is too steep, they will lose speed and may not make it to the top. However, if the arc of the ramp is too shallow, the skateboarders will not get enough height to perform their tricks. So, the skateboarders must design their ramps with the perfect arc to give them the right amount of speed and the right amount of height.

These are just a few examples of the many different ways geometry is used in everyday life. The next time you are walking down the street, look around you—how many examples of geometry do you see?

GEOMETRY ALL AROUND US

Generalizations

B3

Write at least three generalizations about geometry and your everyday life.

Classifications

B2

Study your list from B1. Classify the examples into categories you create. You may not have a "miscellaneous" or "other" category.

Details

B1

Look around you. List as many examples of geometry as you can in 2 minutes. (You should have at least 25 examples.)

Theme/Concept

C3

What is the main idea of "Geometry All Around Us"?
Justify your answer.

Inference

C2

Based on the text, what inferences can
you make about the use of geometry?

Literary Elements

C1

An architect's use of geometry might be characterized as design and a farmer's use of geometry might be characterized as agricultural. How might a skateboarder's use of geometry be characterized? Use evidence from the text to support your answer.

GEOMETRY ALL AROUND US

The Industrial Revolution

The Industrial Revolution began in Great Britain during the late 18th century and early 19th century. During the Revolution, manual labor was replaced by industry, manufacturing, and machinery. There also were dramatic changes in technology, socioeconomics, and culture.

The causes of the Industrial Revolution are still being debated. One theory states that in the 17th century, the borders of Great Britain were better controlled, there was less disease coming into the country from surrounding areas, and more children were living past infancy. All of these conditions led to an increased workforce without enough agricultural work for everyone. Therefore, people began "cottage industries" such as weaving, lace making, and sewing in their homes. Then, in 1701, Jethro Tull invented the seed drill. When farmers used the seed drill, more seeds took root, which led to larger crops, particularly of cotton. As the amount of cotton increased, the demand for products made from cotton also increased. Shortly, the demand for cotton products far exceeded the cottage industries' ability to supply these products. There was a demand for more efficient means of weaving and sewing. According to this theory, then, the Industrial Revolution began in the textile industry to meet the demands of products made from the increased cotton supply.

Another theory cites the expansion of colonial territories, such as America, as the cause of the Industrial Revolution. Expanding territories like America were demanding products from Great Britain. This demand led to the need for more efficient means of production, which then led to the Revolution.

A third theory links the Industrial Revolution to the Scientific Revolution that took place during the 16th century. The Scientific Revolution sparked many inventions, including the steam engine, which made the Industrial Revolution possible.

Although there may be disagreement over the causes of the Industrial Revolution, there certainly is no debate about the many important innovations during this time period, especially in the textile industry. These innovations included the flying shuttle, invented by a watchmaker, which allowed weavers to weave cotton more quickly. Once the weavers were able to work more quickly, the spinners could not keep up with them. In 1764, James Hargreaves won a contest with his invention, the spinning Jenny, which allowed spinners to spin 6–8 threads at once rather than just one thread. Later versions of the spinning Jenny could spin as many as 80 threads at once!

In 1769, Richard Arkwright made it possible for spinners to work even faster. He invented the water frame, which used water power to operate spinning wheels, further increasing the speed of the production process. With the water frame, multiple machines could spin at once with just one person overseeing them all; each machine did not need a person operating it. Then, in 1785, Edmund Cartwright invented the power loom, which increased the speed of weaving so the weavers could keep up with the spinners.

As a final bonus, Eli Whitney, who lived in America, invented the cotton gin in 1793. The cotton gin removed seeds from cotton, which was at this point the most time-consuming element of textile production. With this final addition, the process was streamlined and the production of textiles officially became an industry.

Generalizations

B3

Write at least three generalizations about the Industrial Revolution and how it relates to the modern world.

Classifications

B2

Look at your list from B1. Classify each item on your list into a category. You may not have a miscellaneous or other category.

Details

B1

List at least 15–20 ways the Industrial Revolution affected the modern world.

THE INDUSTRIAL REVOLUTION

Name: _____ Date: _____

Theme/Concept

C3

What is the main idea of the selection "The Industrial Revolution?" Write a new title for the selection that better represents its main idea.

Inference

C2

Which of the three theories about the beginning of the Industrial Revolution is best supported by evidence? Explain your answer using details from the text.

Literary Elements

C1

How would you characterize men like Richard Arkwright, Edmund Cartwright, and Eli Whitney? Use details from the text to support your answer.

What's the Chance?

Have you ever tried to determine what your chances were of rolling a 6 with a pair of dice? Or what your chances were of a penny landing on heads versus tails? All of these questions can be answered with a math strategy known as *probability*.

Probability is the measure of how likely an event is to occur based on the number of ways the event could occur and the total number of possible outcomes. Confusing? Let's review some words that are related to probability and then look at an example. Before you can understand probability, you need to know what experiment, outcome, and event mean in relation to it. An *experiment* is a situation involving chance that leads to outcomes. An *outcome* is the result of a single trial. An *event* is one or more outcomes. OK, now let's look at an example.

Imagine you are rolling a die (that's singular for dice). This is your experiment—you cannot control what number the die will land on, therefore you are involved in a situation dealing with chance. What is the probability that your die will land on the number 3? Landing on the number 3 would be an outcome or the result of a single trial or roll. How many other possible outcomes are there?

Well, you could land on 1, 2, 4, 5, or 6, so there are 5 other possible outcomes. How many total possible outcomes are there? The total number of possible outcomes is the same as the total of numbers on the die, or six. So, if there is only one outcome that will result in you rolling a 3 and there are six total outcomes, then the chances of you rolling a 3 are 1 in 6 or $\frac{1}{6}$. Make sense?

Let's look at another example. Imagine there are four marbles in a bag. One marble is yellow, one is blue, one is green, and one is red. When you pull a marble out of the bag, how many possible outcomes are there? That's right! There are four possible outcomes because there are four different colors. Now, what are your chances of pulling a red marble out of the bag? Only one outcome will lead to a red marble coming out of the bag, so the

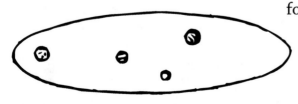

chances of you drawing a red marble are 1 in 4 or $^1/_4$. The same probability also would apply to the yellow, blue, and green marbles.

Both of these examples are of probability scenarios with equally likely outcomes. When rolling a die, you are equally likely to roll a 4 as you are to roll a 2. When drawing a marble out of the bag, you are equally likely to draw one color as another. Sometimes, though, situations involving probability do not have equally likely outcomes. Probability is considered not equally likely if there is a chance that one outcome will occur more or less frequently than another outcome. For example, imagine you have a bag with six blue candies and three red candies. Are you more likely to draw a blue candy or a red candy? First, let's determine how many total outcomes there are. This number will be the same as the total number of candies, or nine. Now, how many outcomes will result in you pulling a blue candy out of the bag? Six outcomes result in a blue candy, so the probability of you getting a blue candy is 6 out of 9 or $^6/_9$. The chances of you getting a red candy are 3 out of 9 or $^3/_9$ because there are only 3 red candies. In this example, it is more likely that you will draw a blue candy than a red candy. Therefore, the probability of these events occurring is not equally likely.

Theme/Concept

C3

What is the main idea of "What's the Chance?" Use evidence from the text to support your answer.

Inference

C2

If P = probability, A = event A, and B = event B, what inferences can you make about the following mathematical sentences?

1. $P(A) > P(B)$

2. $P(A) = P(B)$

3. $P(A) < P(B)$

Literary Elements

C1

If probability were a person, what kind of person would it be? Describe probability. Be sure to include details from the text to support your description.

WHAT'S THE CHANCE?

Creative Synthesis

D3

Write a math word problem that requires the use of probability to solve.

Summarizing

D2

In three sentences or less, describe the differences between equally likely and not equally likely probability.

Paraphrasing

D1

Rewrite the following statement in your own words:

"Probability is the measure of how likely an event is to occur based on the number of ways the event could occur and the total number of possible outcomes."

WHAT'S THE CHANCE?

A World of Resources

Our world is full of many natural resources that people use each and every day. Some examples of natural resources include air, solar energy, aluminum, natural gas, coal, trees, fish, farm animals, and crops. Natural resources can be classified into three different categories: renewable, flow, and nonrenewable.

Renewable natural resources are living resources like fish, deer, trees, and coffee that can grow back or renew themselves with time. In order for a resource to be renewable, the rate of consumption of the resource cannot exceed the amount of time it takes for the resource to replace itself. Metals are an exception to this rule. Metals cannot renew themselves, but they still are considered renewable resources because they can be recycled and reused. Metals, like the aluminum used for soda cans, are not destroyed during the production cycle. Because they are not destroyed, metals are easily melted down and used again and again.

Flow natural resources also are renewable. Unlike renewable resources, though, flow resources do not require time to replenish themselves. Air, water, wind, tides, and solar energy all are examples of flow resources. There is an endless supply of these types of natural resources.

Nonrenewable natural resources are resources that cannot be remade or regrown. Or, if they can be replenished, they cannot be replenished as quickly as the rate of consumption demands. For example, fossil fuels such as coal, natural gas, and petroleum are nonrenewable resources. Fossil fuels can replenish themselves, but the process takes thousands of years. People cannot wait thousands of years for more coal, natural gas, or petroleum. Therefore, these kinds of natural resources are available in limited quantities and considered nonrenewable.

Another way to classify natural resources is by their matter state. Resources can be solid, liquid, or gas. Examples include trees for solid matter, tides for liquid matter, and air for gas matter.

Natural resources also can be classified as organic or inorganic. Organic natural resources are resources that are living or were once living. Organic resources, such as trees, animals, and crops can live and die. Any resource containing carbon, a byproduct of living organisms, is considered organic. Inorganic resources are resources that are nonliving, such as rocks, water, and air.

Sometimes, we take natural resources for granted because they are everywhere. We forget how important these natural resources are to the way we live our lives. We must all make an effort to appreciate and protect our Earth's natural resources.

Consequences and Implications

A3

What would be the consequences of using all of the Earth's nonrenewable resources? Give an example to explain your answer.

Cause and Effect

A2

What would be the effect of humans consuming, or using, a renewable resource at a faster rate than it can replenish itself? Use evidence from the text to support your answer.

Sequencing

A1

List the order in which classification of natural resources was discussed in the text.

A WORLD OF RESOURCES

Name: _____ Date: _____

Generalizations

B3

Write at least three generalizations about natural resources based on your list and your classifications.

Classifications

B2

Using the classifications discussed in the text, classify the natural resources on your list.

Details

B1

List as many natural resources as you can think of in 2 minutes. (List at least 25.)

A WORLD OF RESOURCES

Pre- and Postassessments and Exemplars

Appendix A contains the pre- and postassessment readings and answer forms, as well as a rubric for scoring the assessments. The preassessment should be administered before any work with *Jacob's Ladder 1* is conducted. After all readings and questions have been answered, the postassessment can be given to track student improvement on the ladder skill sets. Included in this appendix are example answers for both the pre- and postassessments. The answers are taken from student responses given during the piloting of this curriculum.

Third-Grade Pretest:
The Fox and the Leopard

Please read the story "The Fox and The Leopard" below. Then, answer the four questions related to the story.

The Fox and the Leopard
(Originally told by Aesop)

The Fox and the Leopard disputed which was the more beautiful of the two. The Leopard exhibited one by one the various spots that decorated his skin. But the Fox, interrupting him, said, "And how much more beautiful than you am I, who am decorated, not in body but in mind."

1. What do you think would have happened if the fox looked like the leopard? Provide evidence from the story to defend your answer.

_____

_____

_____

_____

_____

_____

2. What does the fox mean when he says, "And how much more beautiful than you am I, who am decorated, not in body, but in mind"? Provide evidence from the story to defend your answer.

_____

_____

_____

_____

_____

_____

3. What is the moral of this story? Give a reason why you think so.

_____

_____

_____

_____

_____

_____

4. Create a new title for this fable. Give a reason why your title is better than the original title.

_____

_____

_____

_____

_____

_____

Name: _____ Date: _____

Third-Grade Posttest:
The Frogs and the Well

Please read the story "The Frogs and the Well" below. Then, answer the four questions related to the story.

The Frogs and the Well
(Originally told by Aesop)

Two frogs lived together in a marsh. But one hot summer the marsh dried up, and they left it to look for another place to live in: for frogs like damp places if they can get them. By and by they came to a deep well, and one of them looked down into it, and said to the other, "This looks a nice cool place. Let us jump in and settle here." But the other, who had a wiser head on his shoulders, replied, "Not so fast, my friend. Supposing this well dried up like the marsh, how should we get out again?"

1. What do you think would have happened if the frogs jumped in the well? Provide evidence from the story to defend your answer.

_____

_____

_____

_____

_____

_____

2. The wise frog said, "Not so fast, my friend. Supposing this well dried up like the marsh, how should we get out again?" What made this question so important for the frog to ask? Provide evidence from the story to defend your answer.

_____

_____

_____

_____

_____

3. What is the moral of this story? Give a reason why you think so.

_____

_____

_____

_____

_____

4. Create a new title for this fable. Give a reason why your title is better than the original title.

_____

_____

_____

_____

_____

Assessment Scoring Rubric

Question	Points				
	0	1	2	3	4
1 **Implications and Consequences** **(Ladder A)**	Provides no response or response is inappropriate to the task demand	Limited, vague, inaccurate; rewords the prompt or copies from text	Response is accurate and makes sense but does not adequately address all components of the question or provide rationale from text	Response is accurate; answers all parts of the question; provides a rationale that justifies answer	Response is well written, specific, insightful; answers all parts of the questions, offers substantial support, and incorporates evidence from the text
2 **Inference** **(Ladder C)**	Provides no response or response is inappropriate to the task demand	Limited, vague, inaccurate; rewords the prompt or copies from text	Accurate response but literal interpretation with no support from the text	Interpretive response with limited support from the text	Insightful, interpretive, well-written response with substantial support from the text
3 Theme/ **Generalization** **(Ladders B and C)**	Provides no response or response is inappropriate to the task demand	Limited, vague, inaccurate; rewords the prompt or copies from text	Literal description of the story without explaining the theme; no reasons why	Valid, interpretive response with limited reasoning from the text	Insightful, interpretive response with substantial justification or reasoning
4 **Creative Synthesis** **(Ladder D)**	Provides no response or response is inappropriate to the task demand	Limited, vague, inaccurate; rewords the prompt or copies from text	Appropriate but literal title with no attempt to support	Interpretive title with limited reasoning or justification	Insightful title, interpretive, and extensive justification or reasoning

Example Answers

Third-Grade Pretest: The Fox and the Leopard

Note. These answers are based on student responses and teacher ratings from field trials conducted by the Center for Gifted Education. The answers have not been changed from the original student response.

1. **What do you think would have happened if the fox looked like the leopard? Provide evidence from the story to defend your answer.**

   1-point responses might include:

   - They would be friends.
   - The leopard would be really mad.
   - They would both look the same.

   2-point responses might include:

   - I think if the fox looked like the leopard they would fight over whose spots looked better.
   - Then the leopard would have thought he was still the most beautiful.
   - The leopard wouldn't start a fight.

   3-point responses might include:

   - They wouldn't fight anymore because they would look the same.
   - The fox would win because he looks the same and is the smartest.
   - They wouldn't care who was most beautiful only who was the smartest.

   4-point responses might include:

   - The fox would win the dispute because he is most beautiful with spots decorating his skin and he is smart.
   - They wouldn't have even started fighting because they both had spots decorating their skin so they looked the same.
   - They wouldn't care about being beautiful on the outside anymore. They would only care about who was the most beautiful on the inside in their minds.

2. **What does the fox mean when he says, "And how much more beautiful than you am I, who am decorated, not in body, but in mind"? Provide evidence from the story to defend your answer.**

1-point responses might include:

- The fox means that the leopard is smarter than him.
- He is decorated in mind but not body.
- The fox was being jealous.

2-point responses might include:

- The fox means he is smarter than leopard.
- He meant he may not be as pretty but he is smarter.
- The fox means that his mind is more beautiful than the leopard.

3-point responses might include:

- He means that the leopard is more pretty on the outside but the fox is more wise.
- The fox meant that the leopard was being selfish and he meant that it does not matter how you look on the outside but what matters is how you act on the inside.
- He meant that it's better to be smart than to be beautiful.

4-point responses might include:

- The fox means he's smart and better than the leopard because he said he was decorated in the mind.
- The fox means he's more beautiful than the fox because he is smarter and that's more important than having pretty spots decorating your skin.
- He means that it's better to be smart than to just be beautiful on the outside. Because he said he is more beautiful because he is decorated "not in body but in mind."

3. **What is the moral of this story? Give a reason why you think so.**

1-point responses might include:

- It is OK to look better than somebody else.
- The moral is that two animals argue over who is more beautiful.
- The moral of the story is the fox is more beautiful.

2-point responses might include:

- I think the lesson of this story is not to argue over who is more beautiful.

- The lesson is everyone can be beautiful.

- You shouldn't brag about your beauty.

3-point responses might include:

- I think the moral of the story is that it doesn't matter if you don't look good it is more important to be smart.

- The moral teaches that people are not just beautiful on the outside, they are beautiful on the inside too.

- The moral is beauty is only skin deep.

4-point responses might include:

- The moral of the story is that it is more important to be smart than to be pretty. Like when the fox said that he is more beautiful than the leopard because he's decorated in mind.

- The lesson is it is better to be smart and decorated in mind like the fox than to just be pretty like the leopard.

- The moral of the story is that you shouldn't show off how good you look, like when the leopard showed off his spots one by one to the fox. It is more important to be beautiful on the inside.

4. **Create a new title for this fable. Give a reason why your title is better than the original title.**

1-point responses might include:

- The Leopard and the Fox.

- My title is The Cow and the Chicken because I don't like foxes and leopards.

- The Two Animals.

2-point responses might include:

- The Fox and the Leopard Fighting. I think mine is better because it has more words.

- The Spotted Leopard and the Thoughtful Fox.

- My title is The Smart Fox and the Beautiful Leopard.

3-point responses might include:

- <u>The Argument</u> because the fox and the leopard are arguing.

- <u>The Fox and the Leopard Fight</u>. I think it is better because they are fighting about who is more beautiful.

- <u>Who Is More Beautiful</u>? Because the fox and the leopard are trying to prove who is more beautiful.

4-point responses might include:

- <u>The Inside Counts</u>. I think this is a good title because it's the moral of the story and the fox is right, his brain is better than his body.

- <u>Beauty's Only Skin Deep</u>. This is a better title because it tells the moral of the story. The fox shows that just being beautiful on the outside isn't as good as being beautiful on the inside.

- <u>Beautiful in Mind.</u> This title is good because it shows what the fox said about how being beautiful in mind is better than just having decorated skin.

Example Answers

Third-Grade Posttest: The Frogs and the Well

Note. These answers are based on student responses and teacher ratings from field trials conducted by the Center for Gifted Education. The answers have not been changed from the original student response.

1. **What do you think would have happened if the frogs jumped in the well? Provide evidence from the story to defend your answer.**

   1-point responses might include:

   - I think that there could have been a real mean frog in the well.
   - I think the frogs would have gone to look for another home because one frog said, not so fast my friend. Supposing the well was dry like the marsh.
   - I think if they jumped in they would be nice and cool.

   2-point responses might include:

   - If the frogs jumped in the well the frog could die in the well.
   - They might have never gotten out of the well.
   - They would have been stuck in the well forever.

   3-point responses might include:

   - I think the frog would have not been able to get out of the well. My evidence is that the other frog warned them that the well might dry up.
   - If the frogs jumped in the well they would have just realized that when the well dries up they would not be able to get out and they would have no water and they would die.
   - I think the well would have dried up and they would not be able to get out because the wise frog told him this.

   4-point responses might include:

   - If the frogs jumped in the well another hot day might come and dry up the well like the marsh and the frogs wouldn't be able to get out of the well because it's so far down.
   - I think if the frogs jumped in the well the two little frogs will get stuck in the well. In the story the wise frog said how would we get out again?

- I think if the frogs would have jumped in the well they really would not have been able to get out because no frog can jump out of such a deep place if the water dried up. My evidence from the story is the first frog said, "Not so fast my friend. Supposing this well dried up like the marsh, how should we get out again?"

2. **The wise frog said, "Not so fast, my friend. Supposing this well dried up like the marsh, how should we get out again?" What made this question so important for the frog to ask? Provide evidence from the story to defend your answer.**

1-point responses might include:

- It was important that the frog said "Not so fast" because the frog knew that there was something in the well.

- The question is important because the wise frog said it.

- But the other frog who had a wiser head on his shoulders replied not so fast my friend.

2-point responses might include:

- I think that the question was important because it made the not wise frog think a little bit.

- I think he just said it to warn the other frog that said "let's jump in."

- It was so important because it could save the other frogs life.

3-point responses might include:

- It was so important for the wise frog to ask because if they jumped in they could not get out. In the story it said it was a deep well.

- This question was important to the story because the wise frog was actually trying to teach the other frog a lesson.

- It was so important the frog asked it because he did not want to die in the well and that is why the frog asked that important question.

4-point responses might include:

- This was important for the frog to ask because the wise one knew that if they jumped in it could dry up like the marsh and they would not be able to get out. The other one was thinking let's jump in.

- This was so important for the wise frog to ask because it made his friend stop and think before he jumped into the deep well. If he didn't ask they could be stuck in the well forever because it could dry up like the marsh and they couldn't get out again.

- It was important because it made his friend think about how they would get out before they jumped in. If he didn't they could have been stuck in the well if it dried up and never been able to get out again.

3. **What is the moral of this story? Give a reason why you think so.**

1-point responses might include:

- The frogs had to leave the marsh because it is dried up.

- I think the moral of the story is maybe the wise frog should have jumped in.

- The moral of the story is not to jump into the well.

2-point responses might include:

- The moral of the story is that the frog that was not smart thought that it was smart to move into the well but the other said no, what if it dries up like the marsh did.

- The moral of the story is that if you move out of your house and want a new one you should ask somebody about the house.

- The moral of the story is not to live somewhere if you know it's going to dry up quickly.

3-point responses might include:

- Think before you act.

- You should think twice before you do something.

- The moral of this story is to think before you do stuff, because if you're not careful you could die or get hurt.

4-point responses might include:

- I think the moral of this story is to think before you act, because in the story the marsh dried up from the sun and if they had moved into the well without thinking a hot day could come up again and the sun could dry up the cool water in the well and they would be stuck.

- The moral of this story is think before you act. If the frogs jumped in the well without thinking they would be stuck. The wise frog thought first.

- The lesson of this story is if something looks safe that does not mean it is safe. I think that because the one frog thought that it looked safe but the wise one gave a reason why they should not go in there.

4. **Create a new title for this fable. Give a reason why your title is better than the original title.**

1-point responses might include:

- <u>The Frogs Pond is Dried Up</u>.

- <u>The Frogs and the Pond</u>. I think this is better.

- <u>How the Frog Got in the Well</u> because the frog is in the well.

2-point responses might include:

- <u>The Two Frogs That Went to a Well</u>.

- <u>The Frogs, the Marsh, and the Well</u>.

- I think the title should be <u>Finding a Home</u>.

3-point responses might include:

- <u>The Frogs' Problem</u>. I think this title is better than the original because the frogs have a problem in the story.

- <u>The Foolish Frog</u> is a better title because the frog almost jumped into the well and that would be foolish.

- I think that the title of this story should be, <u>Think, Think, and Think Before You Do Something</u> because you should always think before you do something.

4-point responses might include:

- <u>The Wise Frog</u>. This would be a good title because if the wise frog would not have said, not so fast my friend, the other frog might have lost his life.

- <u>Think Before You Do Something</u>. That is a better title because the frogs had to stop [and] think before they jumped in the well. If they didn't they could have been stuck in the well.

- I think <u>Be Wise Little Frog</u> should be the title because the one frog wanted to go live in the well but his brother said no because it might dry up and they couldn't get out.

APPENDIX
B

Record-Keeping Forms/Documents

Appendix B contains three record-keeping forms and documents:

1. *Brainstorming/Answer Sheet*: This should be given to students for completion after reading a selection so that they may jot ideas or questions about the selection they read prior to participating in discussion. The purpose of this sheet is to capture students' thoughts and ideas generated after individually reading a text. This sheet serves as a guide for student preparedness so that the student is ready to share ideas in group discussion.

2. *Reflection Page*: This form may be completed by the student after group or class discussion on the readings. The reflection page is designed as a metacognitive approach to help students reflect on their strengths and weaknesses and to promote process skills. After discussion, students use the reflection page to record new ideas that were generated by others' comments and ideas.

3. *Classroom Diagnostic Form*: This form is for teachers and is designed to aid them in keeping track of the progress and skill mastery of their students. With this chart, teachers can record student progress in relation to each ladder skill within a genre and select additional ladders and story selections based on student needs.

Brainstorming/Answer Sheet

Use this form to brainstorm thoughts and ideas about the readings and ladder questions before discussing with a partner.

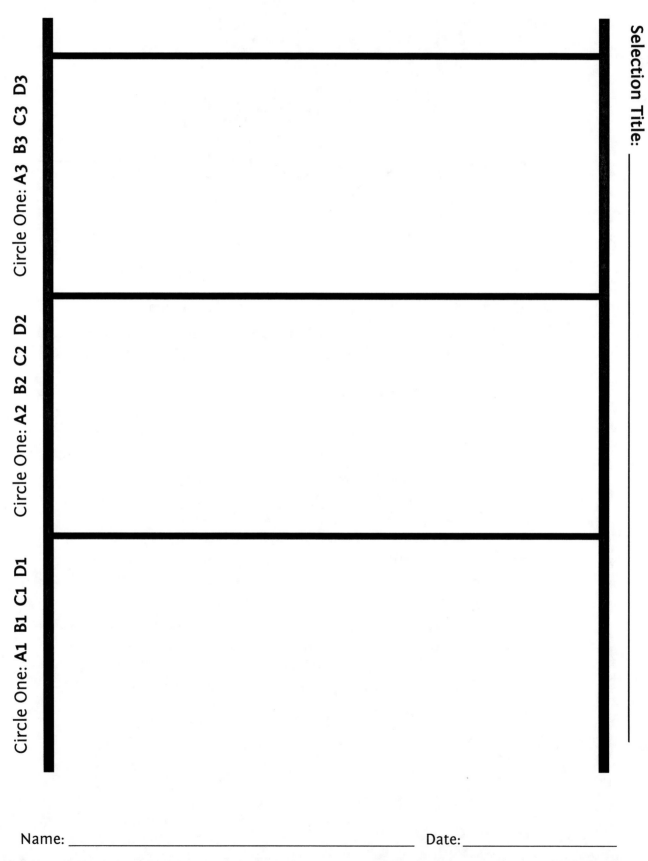

Selection Title: _____

Circle One: **A3 B3 C3 D3**

Circle One: **A2 B2 C2 D2**

Circle One: **A1 B1 C1 D1**

Name: _____ Date: _____

Name: _____ Date: _____

My Reflection on
Today's Reading and Discussion

Selection Title: _____

What I did well:

_____

_____

_____

_____

What I learned:

_____

_____

_____

_____

New ideas I have after discussion:

_____

_____

_____

_____

Next time I need to:

_____

_____

_____

_____

Classroom Diagnostic Form

Short Stories

Use this document to record student completion of ladder sets with the assessment of work.

0 = Needs Improvement   1 = Satisfactory   2 = Exceeds Expectations

Student Name	The Ant and the Dove		The Crow and the Pitcher		Daedalus and Icarus		The Dog and His Reflection		The Fisherman and His Wife
	A	B	A	C	A	C	A	C	A

Classroom Diagnostic Form

Short Stories

Use this document to record student completion of ladder sets with the assessment of work.

0 = Needs Improvement   1 = Satisfactory   2 = Exceeds Expectations

Student Name	The Judge		The Lion and the Gnat		The Mice in Council		The North Wind and the Sun		The Tap Dancer	
	A		A	C	A	C	A	B	A	C

Classroom Diagnostic Form
Poetry

Use this document to record student completion of ladder sets with the assessment of work.

0 = Needs Improvement   1 = Satisfactory   2 = Exceeds Expectations

Student Name	Artist	City	Delilah	Fog	Imagination	Remember-ing	A Rose	Under My Bed	Windy Nights	Winter Horses
	C	C	C	B	B	C	A	B	A	C

Classroom Diagnostic Form
Nonfiction

Use this document to record student completion of ladder sets with the assessment of work.

0 = Needs Improvement   1 = Satisfactory   2 = Exceeds Expectations

Student Name	Ancient Rome		The Circle of Life		Geometry All Around Us		The Industrial Revolution		What's the Chance?		A World of Resources	
	A	D	A	D	B	C	B	C	C	D	A	B

Answer Key

This key includes example answers for all ladder questions. Sample answers were generated to illustrate the skills students should be mastering. However, because the questions are open-ended and designed to promote discussion, these answers should only be used as a guide. Variations and original thought should be valued and rewarded.

Short Stories Answer Key

These are suggested answers only. Answers will vary.

The Ant and the Dove

Ladder Set A

A1. 1. The ant fell in the rapidly moving stream; 2. The dove dropped a leaf into the stream; 3. The ant crawled on the leaf; 4. A hunter took aim at the dove; 5. The ant bit the hunter; 6. The hunter screamed; 7. The dove flew away.

A2.

Cause	Effect
Ant was thirsty	Went to the stream's edge and fell in
Dove dropped a leaf	The ant was able to get back to shore
Ant bit the hunter	The dove also was able to escape harm

A3. Because the dove was willing to help the ant, the ant later returned the favor. Therefore, the dove saved his own life by dropping the leaf for the ant.

Ladder Set B

B1. Thirsty ant; rapidly moving stream; plucked a leaf; struggling ant; drew his bow; pierced his target; stung him; cried out in pain; dove flew away.

B2.

Good Turn	Why?
Dove dropped the leaf	Because it gave the ant something to use to float back to shore
Ant bit the hunter	Because the hunter's cry of pain warned the dove who was then able to fly away

B3. Do unto others as you would have them do unto you. OR I'll scratch your back if you'll scratch mine.

The Crow and the Pitcher

Ladder Set A

A1. 1. He put his beak into the pitcher; 2. He tried harder to stick his beak deeper into the pitcher; 3. He dropped pebbles into the pitcher; 4. He saw the water rising and was able to drink it.

A2. The displacement of water by the pebbles caused the water to become available to the crow. The overall effect was that the crow's life was saved.

A3.
- He would have never gotten to drink any water and he probably would have died of thirst.

- He might have been able to find water somewhere else, but there were no guarantees.

- The water would have spilled and soaked into the ground.

- He might have died of thirst before the rain came.

Ladder Set C

C1. The crow was very creative and persistent. He knew he needed water and he was not willing to give up. He was creative because he figured out how to make the water come to him. Answers for the final question will vary. One example might be: The crow reminds me of the three little pigs. The third little pig decides to build his house out of bricks and works very hard, without giving up, until his house is finished. The three little pigs also are creative because of the way they catch the wolf in the pot at the bottom of the chimney. The crow and the three little pigs are different because they had each other and could develop a plan together. The crow had to save himself all on his own.

C2. Hard work and persistence made the crow successful. His plan worked because he kept adding pebbles until he could see the water. He believed in his plan and persisted even though he did not get immediate results.

C3. The main idea of this story is to never give up. If you work hard enough and think you will succeed, eventually you will.

Daedalus and Icarus

Ladder Set A

A1. 1. Daedalus was given the job of designing a new palace with a secret underground labyrinth for the king of Crete; 2. The king locked Daedalus and Icarus in the highest tower; 3. Daedalus patiently collected bird feathers and old candle wax; 4. Daedalus made two pairs of wings using the feathers and wax; 5. Daedalus told Icarus not to fly too high, and they escaped the palace; 6. Icarus flew too close to the sun, the wax on his wings melted, and he fell to the sea.

A2. Icarus fell into the sea because he did not listen to his father.

A3. This myth reminded me to listen to my parents, especially when safety is concerned. It also should remind society to take the advice of other people who know more about a situation than they do.

Ladder Set C

C1.

Character	Relationship
Daedalus	Father to Icarus, employee to king of Crete
Icarus	Son of Daedalus
King of Crete	King and the boss of Daedalus and Icarus

- The story took place in Ancient Greece on the Island of Crete.

C2. Icarus did not obey his father because he felt such exhilarating freedom while flying. He was overcome by the desire to fly higher that he forgot about his father's warning.

C3.

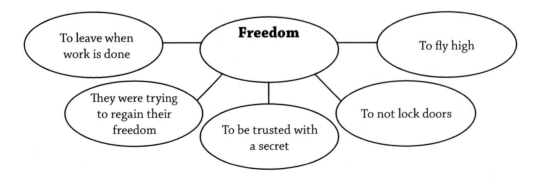

The Dog and His Reflection

Ladder Set A

A1. 1. The butcher throws the dog a bone; 2. The dog sees himself in the water as he is crossing the bridge; 3. He thinks his reflection is another dog with a bigger bone and jumps at it; 4. He almost drowns, but manages to make it to shore; 5. He thinks about the bone he lost and what a silly dog he had been.

A2.
- The dog lost his bone because he tried to attack the other dog (his own reflection) to get what he thought was a bigger bone.
- The effect of losing his bone was to make the dog realize how foolish and greedy he had been.
- Illustrations will vary. The dog should be happier, even arrogant, in the first picture and sad or self-reproaching in the second drawing.

A3.
- He lost his bone and nearly drowned.
- He lost his bone, his pride, his arrogance, his greed, his dinner, his spontaneity, and so forth.
- The next time he sees his reflection he will realize it is an image of himself and not another dog.

Ladder Set C

C1.

Qualities	Positive	Negative
Self-confidence	He feels good about himself	He thought he deserved and could get a bigger, better bone
Greed		He nearly died trying to get a bigger bone
Strength	He was able to save himself from drowning	

C2. I can infer that the dog wanted the bigger bone he thought he saw in the mouth of the other dog. I can also infer that he did not like the idea of another dog having a bigger bone than he had.

C3. The story tells us not to be greedy. We should appreciate what we have, especially when it is enough. We should not want what other people have, but instead should be happy with what we have.

The Fisherman and His Wife

Ladder Set A

A1. 1. The fisherman caught an enchanted fish; 2.The wife told the fisherman he should have asked the fish to grant him a wish; 3. The wife wanted a cottage; 4.The sea was green and yellow; 5. The wife wanted to be emperor; 6. The sea was black and the wind was blowing; 7. The wife was returned to the cottage in which she and the fisherman originally lived.

A2. Every time the wife wished for something else, the fisherman would agree to ask the fish. But every time he came back from getting her wish granted, his wife still was not happy. Every time he got one of her wishes granted, she would immediately want something else.

A3. Because the wife was never satisfied with what she had, she eventually had nothing at all.

The Judge

Ladder Set A

A1. ▪ The mice went to the lion for help first and to the monkey for help second.

▪ 1. He agreed to help the mice; 2. He ate the largest piece of cheese; 3. He weighed the cheese again; 4. He told the mice they would fight with and the King would be angry; 5. He ate all the cheese.

A2. ▪ The lion told the mice that many new problems might arise if they asked the monkey for help rather than settling their argument themselves.

▪ After the monkey ate part of the big piece of cheese, it became smaller than the small piece of cheese. Then, the monkey ate some of the new big piece of cheese. Eventually, the monkey ate all of the cheese and the mice did not get any.

A3. ▪ The lion knew the monkey would trick the mice. I know the lion knew because he told the mice that more problems might come up if they asked the monkey for help. He tried to convince the mice to settle their own differences without the help of anyone else.

▪ The moral of the story is to settle arguments with your friends on your own rather than asking someone else to solve your problems for you. If the mice had been able to agree on how to divide the cheese then they would have gotten to eat it. Instead, the monkey ate all of the cheese because the mice could not solve their own argument.

The Lion and the Gnat

Ladder Set A

A1. Drawings will vary.

A2. The gnat, the small character, got caught in the spider web because he was preoccupied with wanting to tell the whole world that he had defeated the lion.

A3. ▪ One of the consequences of being smaller than other creatures is that you feel like you need to prove yourself to the bigger creatures by trying to beat them.

▪ One of the consequences of being larger than other creatures makes you think you cannot be defeated by creatures smaller than you.

▪ One of the consequences of being clever is that you often can outsmart other people, but also can get too carried away by outsmarting them.

▪ One of the consequences of being too proud is that you forget to look out for yourself and others; you think you are so perfect that you cannot make any mistakes.

C1.

Characters	Similarities	Differences
Gnat	Pride; gets defeated; thinks he is better than the other	Gnat is small, gets defeated by the spider
Lion	Pride; gets defeated; thinks he is better than the other	Lion is big, gets defeated by the gnat

C2. I can tell the gnat was proud because he told the lion he was not afraid of him. I also know he was proud because he flew away quickly to tell everyone that he had defeated the lion.

C3. The main idea of the story is that you should be kind to others and you should not take pride in defeating others. (Stories will vary.)

The Mice in Council

Ladder Set A

A1. 1. Wait until the cat is asleep; 2. Tiptoe out of the mouse hole; 3. Carefully place the bell on a string around the cat's neck; 4. Run as fast as they can back into the mouse hole.

A2.

In the story, the cat *caused*:	The *effect* was that the mice:
The mice to be scared	Wanted to get rid of the cat
The mice to develop ideas for getting rid of the cat	One mouse suggested putting a bell around the cat's neck

A3. Older is wiser. (The older mouse was the wise one who warned against the dangers of trying to put a bell around the cat's neck.)

Ladder Set B

B1.

	Qualities	Habits
Cats	Hunters	They like to chase and catch mice
Mice	Scavengers	They like to scuttle around looking for crumbs and cheese

B2. Although putting a bell around the cat's neck would allow the mice to know when the cat was coming, it also would mean that a mouse would have to get very close to the cat. The mouse who took on this job could very easily be caught. So, the question is asking whether or not there is a mouse that would be willing to sacrifice himself for the good of the other mice.

B3. This story teaches us that by working together groups can develop solutions for problems. It also reminds us that sometimes a member of a group has to take chances in order to benefit the entire group.

The North Wind and the Sun

Ladder Set A

A1. The first time the wind blew the man wrapped his coat around himself. The second time the wind blew the man held his coat more tightly around himself.

A2. The effect of the wind blowing more forcefully on the traveler was that the traveler pulled his coat more tightly around him instead of taking it off as the wind had wanted.

A3. ▪ The wind tried to use force to blow the man's coat off. Instead, the sun made it seem as if it was the man's decision to take off his coat because he was feeling too warm. The sun's method was better because the decision was placed in the hands of the man—he was not being forced to do something that he may not want to do.

▪ The wind could have blown more gently and made the man think that a nice, pleasant breeze was blowing. Then, the man might have taken off his coat to enjoy the wind's soft caress.

Ladder Set B

B1. ▪ The strength of the wind was his great power and force.

▪ The strength of the sun was her intense heat and awesome light.

▪ The sun was stronger because she chose to use her power in cooperation with the man's desires rather than trying to use her power to force the man to take off his coat.

B2. Answers will vary, but should include specific examples from students' personal experience and/or texts they have read.

B3. It is easier to convince someone using persuasion than power. Power only goes as far as you can force it. Persuasion works in favor of everyone involved.

The Tap Dancer

Ladder Set A

A1. 1. The horse decided to give a tap dancing recital for his friends; 2. The horse's friends laughed at him and said he was not a tap dancer; 3. The horse knew in his heart that he was a good tap dancer and continued to dance for himself.

A2. Because his friends laughed at him, the horse did not give any more recitals. But, he enjoyed dancing so he continued to tap dance for himself. (Stories of own experiences will vary. Comparisons should be between the horse's reactions and the student's reactions.)

A3. If the audience had clapped, the horse might have been able to continue giving recitals. He would be able to continue sharing his love of tap dancing with his friends.

Ladder Set C

C1. The horse possesses a lot of self-confidence. I know he does because even though his friends laughed at him he was not willing to give in to peer pressure and stop doing what he loved.

C2. He practiced all of the fancy steps; he found some flat rocks to dance on so he could hear the tapping noises; he organized a recital for his friends; he took a big bow when the recital was over; and he did not stop dancing just because his friends laughed at him.

C3. We should not give up things we love doing just because someone else does not appreciate our talent.

Poetry Answer Key

These are suggested answers only. Answers will vary.

Artist

Ladder Set C

C1. ▪ Poems will vary.

▪ The sun is like an artist because it uses light and shadows to paint pictures on the leaves and on the ground like an artist uses paint to make pictures with light and shadow on canvas.

▪ Drawings will vary.

C2. The sun cannot paint anymore because all of the leaves have fallen off the trees. It cannot create light and shadow on the leaves because all that remains are branches.

C3. The ideas about nature this poem conveys include nature's appreciation for beauty; nature's ability to create beautiful pictures for us to appreciate; and the idea that the sun might be angry when it cannot create and share beauty.

City

Ladder Set C

C1. ▪ Phrases: spreads its wings; makes a song; singing stones; goes to bed; hanging lights around its head.

▪ The author uses words and phrases to put pictures in my head by describing actions the city performs that make me think about what it looks like when people do these actions.

▪ Illustrations will vary.

C2. ▪ By this stanza the author means that that as night approaches the city is getting ready by "hanging lights," which are really stars. It can be inferred that the city is getting ready for the night.

▪ The answer that best describes this quote is "It is a starry night." Above the city's head would be the sky and the lights that are in the sky at night are stars, so the lights the city is hanging are probably stars.

C3. The title, "City," gives the reader a clue about the main idea of the poem because it identifies the main character in the poem. The city is the one who sings, hangs lights, and goes to bed. These are all actions a character in a story would do. Therefore, the poem is named after the main character in the poem and the character's actions are the main idea of the poem.

Delilah

Ladder Set C

C1. The words ocean, rose, heart, fan, and night sky all present images that are pleasant. A creature with so many pleasant characteristics must be lovable.

C2. ▪ The evidence that is important for identifying Delilah are the features she possesses such as eyes, tongue, nose, tail, and black coat.

▪ Answers will vary. Look for evidence from the poem in answers. A possible answer may include: Delilah is a cat. The features of the tail and the black coat are what distinguish her as a cat rather than a different kind of creature.

C3. Poems will vary.

Fog

Ladder Set B

B1. Illustrations will vary.

B2. Little feet; stealth; cats are very quiet; pouncing; stalking; lingering and watching.

B3. Poems will vary. Students do not necessarily have to choose a pair in the same row. For example, they may choose wind and horse or fire and bird.

Imagination

Ladder Set B

B1. ▪ Pictures may vary, but they must be related to an image from the poem, such as: Fish flying, birds in the ocean, dogs walking people, cats walking dogs, sharks sleeping in a bed, turtles playing with frogs, panda bears in cold Canada, kangaroos wearing boots, and chameleons wearing suits.

▪ Lists will vary. Images should not be redundant (e.g., fish wearing shoes, fish wearing jeans, fish wearing a hat); each image should be unique.

B2. The images should be categorized by similar features. For example, if a student listed fish eating popsicles, rabbits chewing gum, and elephants drinking chocolate milk, he or she may put these images into a category called Animals Eating Extraordinary Things. This category may be similar to other categories because it includes animals. It may be different from other categories because it does not include habitats.

B3.

Generalization	Evidence From the Poem	Evidence From My List
Silly images put things together that are not normally associated with each other. (Students should list at least four generalizations.)	Kangaroos wearing boots	Elephants drinking chocolate milk

Remembering

Ladder Set C

C1. Personification is used in this poem. The cottage exhibits human qualities because it feels lonely and sad. It also remembers times it felt love. These are all human emotions.

C2. ▪ The house feels sad and lonely because the people who used to live in it are gone. The poem talks about the children laughing and singing, but now it is quiet and the house is old. The cottage misses the children being there, which makes it feel sad; it is used to having people in it and that is why it feels lonely.

- Yes, I think the house would like to return to the "days of love." The poem says it will "stand forever / Thinking back on the days of love." If the house could have those days back then it would not have to spend all of its time remembering when it was happier because it would be happy.

C3. The change the house experienced was negative. If it had been a positive change then the house would have been talking about what was happening in the present or what it was looking forward to in the future. Instead, it is so unhappy that all it wants to do is think about the past before the change occurred.

A Rose

Ladder Set A

A1. • The poem begins in summer and ends in spring.

Rose grows → gets old and sick → dies, turns into dust → new rose takes its place

A2. • The rose's pain is caused by the fact that it has to die. I think the pain is intended to be emotional because the rose does not want to leave the Earth yet. The poem talks about all of the time the rose was living and the last two lines indicate that everything is OK once the new rose takes its place.

- The growth of the new rose at the end of the poem makes the tone happier. If the poem had ended with the old rose dying, it would have been very sad. But the new rose growing in its place reminds us that the seasons are cyclical and there is always renewal.

A3. • If it was always summer, then the rose would keep growing and growing forever. If it was always winter then a new rose would never come to take the place of the old rose. If it was always summer, people would always be hot, they would never get to see snow, and their grass would always need watering (so the water bill would be very expensive). If it was always winter, then people would always be cold, they would not get to go to the beach, there would be no swimming pools, and they would have to run the heat all the time (so the electricity bill would be very expensive).

- The poem implies that the natural cycle of living things is good because it helps the world constantly rejuvenate itself. Roses will continue to grow, wither, and die and they will always be replaced by new roses. It gives us hope because we can constantly rejuvenate ourselves and our own lives like nature does.

Under My Bed

Ladder Set B

B1. Answers will vary, but students must support their answers with words and phrases from the text of the poem.

B2. Objects with wings—gives the image of toys, books, and other kid things with bird-like wings
Ribbon of red . . . forms a road—ribbon is being presented as something someone can drive on—a road
Picture is read—books are read, pictures are looked at—this metaphor suggests a merging of the two activities
The mountains are soldiers at attention—presents the image of mountains dressed in uniform, standing straight and tall, waiting to receive commands

B3. Students may choose any of the three options: freedom of expression, creativity, or passion. Explanations of their answers must contain words and/or phrases from the text of the poem.

Windy Nights

Ladder Set A

A1. Whenever, gallop, and by. These words are important to the order of the poem because whenever tells you when the man rides his horse, gallop tells you how he rides his horse, and by tells in what direction and in what pattern he rides his horse. All of these words combined give an image of the sequence of events that occur when the man decides to ride.

A2. The wind causes the man to ride when it is high. It also causes the trees to cry aloud and the ships to be tossed at sea. Other effects that the wind might cause might include a howling sound as it moves between buildings, for rain to fall sideways, for sand to be blown about, and leaves to be churned up.

A3. He is the wind being personified by a man riding the horse. Line 4 reads, "A man goes riding by." The lines later in the poem that use the word "he" are referring to the galloping nature of the blowing wind.

Winter Horses

Ladder Set C

C1. ▪ "A storm approaches / like a band of wild colts"

▪ "twisted tails and / flying forelegs are oak leaves dancing in the breeze"; "shaking manes and flashing heels are just / snowflakes laughing at the wind"; "defiant whinnies are / only the trees shuddering against the cold"; and "frost that clings to the grass is the / lingering dust of their passage."

C2. Phrases like "are only" and "are just" suggest something that is not serious and not permanent. Words like *clinging* suggest something that is holding on for as long as it can.

C3. ▪ Animals and seasons may vary.

▪ Poems and titles will vary. Poems should follow the same structure (similes, metaphors, and rhythm) as "Winter Horses" and should contain references to an animal and a season listed in the chart for C3.

Nonfiction Answer Key

These are suggested answers only. Answers will vary.

Ancient Rome

Ladder Set A

A1. 753 B.C., Romulus and Remus founded Rome (or archaeological evidence dates the beginning of Rome to the 8th century B.C.); between 509 and 501 B.C. the Roman Kingdom became the Roman Republic; in 44 B.C. Julius Caesar was assassinated; Augustus came to power in 31 B.C., beginning the Roman Empire; 96–180 A.D., Roman Empire reached its largest land mass; 293 A.D., Emperor Diocletian split the Empire into eastern and western halves; 395 A.D., Constantine made Constantinople the capital of the Eastern Empire (Byzantine Empire); 410 A.D., Western Roman Empire fell to the Visigoths; 1453 A.D., Byzantine Empire fell to the Ottoman Empire or Mehmet II

A2. Answers will vary. Some possible responses: Civil War; the senate gained too much power and was no longer representing the people; the government was corrupt; the rebellion of the First Triumvirate.

A3. Because of its large size, the Roman Empire could not be controlled by one ruler. The consequences, therefore, were that the Empire was split in half. Because of the split, the Eastern Empire became a different Empire all together. Not long after the split became official with the naming as Constantinople as the capital of the Eastern Empire, the Western Empire was conquered by German Visigoths.

Ladder Set D

D1. Answers will vary. Students must rewrite the statement, not just change a few words.

D2. Answers will vary. Students should include the excessive power of the senate, the rebellion of the First Triumvirate, and the rise of Augustus after many internal struggles for power. Ensure students' answers are three sentences or less and encompass the main ideas of the fall of the Roman Republic and the subsequent rise of the Roman Empire.

D3. Answers will vary. Check students' answers to ensure that the journal entry includes events that are likely to have happened during the era chosen.

The Circle of Life

Ladder Set A

A1. Amphibian: egg, larvae, adult.
Winged insect: egg, larvae, pupae, adult.

A2. The nonwinged insects move to the next stage of development when they shed their exoskeleton. They shed their exoskeleton when they have become too large for it.

A3. Once an amphibian or an insect reaches the final stage of the life cycle, the new adult has the responsibility to continue the life cycle. The adult amphibian or insect must lay eggs to begin the life cycle over again. In order to have this opportunity, it must protect itself, find food to eat, and so forth.

Ladder Set D

D1. Answers will vary. Students must rewrite the statement, not just change a few words.

D2. Answers will vary. Students should mention simple metamorphosis versus complex metamorphosis. They also may mention that winged insects have a distinct pupae stage whereas nonwinged insects do not. Make sure student answers are three sentences or less and encompass the main differences between the two types of insects.

D3. Answers will vary. Student accounts of the amphibian's or insect's experience should be accurate. For example, if a student decides to write about the experience from a salamander's perspective, the salamander should not advance beyond the larval stage of development.

Geometry All Around Us

Ladder Set B

B1. Answers will vary. Check students' list to ensure they include only examples of geometry.

B2. Answers will vary based on what students have included on their lists. Check their classification using the definitions and descriptions included in the text, as well as the definitions of geometrical terms.

B3. Answers will vary. Generalizations should be broad, overarching statements that apply to geometry and its everyday uses.

Ladder Set C

C1. Answers will vary. Some possible responses include recreational, entertainment, sports, and so forth.

C2. Answers will vary. Students should mention that the inference can be made that geometry is very important to the world as we know it. Without geometry, houses might not be symmetrical, farmers might buy too many or too few seeds for their crops, and/or skateboarders may not be able to perform many of their most impressive tricks.

C3. Answers will vary. Students should focus on the prevalence of geometry in the things we see and do every day.

The Industrial Revolution

Ladder Set B

B1. Answers will vary. Depending on the amount of students' prior knowledge, some examples may not be found in the text. Check students' answers to ensure they are related to advances made during the Industrial Revolution.

B2. Answers will vary based on what students have included on their lists. Check that their classifications and categories are logical and appropriately organized.

B3. Answers will vary. Generalizations should be broad, overarching statements that apply to the Industrial Revolution and its impact on our modern world.

Ladder Set C

C1. Answers will vary. Possible answers might include characteristics such as inventive, creative, forward thinking, ahead of their time, intelligent, productive, contributors to the advancement of technology, and so forth.

C2. Answers will vary. Check students' answers for logical support based on the information in the text and, possibly, previous knowledge of the Industrial Revolution.

C3. Answers will vary. Check students' answers for justification related to the details in the text.

What's the Chance?

Ladder Set C

C1. Answers will vary but would include how certain things people do are predictable but people cannot control what happens. They also may describe how people plan events but can't control the outcomes.

C2. $P(A) > P(B)$: The probability of event A occurring is greater than the probability of event B occurring.
$P(A) = P(B)$: Events A and B are equally likely to occur.
$P(A) < P(B)$: The probability of event A occurring is less than the probability of event B occurring.

C3. Answers will vary. Answers should mention that chance can be mathematically predicted through probability. They also should mention equally likely versus not equally likely probability.

Ladder Set D

D1. Answers will vary. Students must rewrite the statement, not just change a few words.

D2. Answers will vary. Students should mention that equally likely probability means that the chances of one outcome occurring are equal to the chances of another outcome. Not equally likely probability means that the chances of one outcome occurring are greater or less than the chances of another outcome. Ensure students' answers are three sentences or less and encompass the main differences between the two types of probability.

D3. Answers will vary. Check students' answers to ensure that the word problem requires probability and uses probability correctly.

A World of Resources

Ladder Set A

A1. Renewable, flow, nonrenewable; answer also may include: states of matter (solid, liquid, gas), organic, inorganic.

A2. Answers will vary. Students should indicate that once a renewable resource is used, it begins to replenish itself. However, if the rate of consumption exceeds the rate of renewal, then we will be in danger of depleting the supply of resources.

A3. Answers will vary. Students should indicate that once a non-renewable resource is gone, it cannot be replenished, or at least not quickly. They also should indicate that people will have to find alternative resources if they exhaust the supply of nonrenewable resources. Some students may mention nonrenewable resources such as gas; if we run out, then we will not be able to use our cars until we find an alternative fuel.

Ladder Set B

B1. Answers will vary. Check students' list to ensure they include only natural resources or that students have indicated how an item on their list is derived from a natural resource.

B2. Answers will vary based on what students have included on their lists. Check their classification using the definitions and descriptions included in the text.

B3. Answers will vary. Generalizations should be broad, overarching statements that apply to all natural resources or to a specific category of natural resources.